A HISTORY TODAY BOOK

# Scotland Revisited

EDITED BY JENNY WORMALD

COLLINS & BROWN

First published in Great Britain in 1991
by Collins & Brown Limited
Mercury House
195 Knightsbridge
London SW7 1RE

A CIP catalogue record for this book
is available from the British Library

ISBN 1 85585 092 3

Typeset by Falcon Graphic Art Ltd, Wallington, Surrey
Printed and bound in Great Britain by The Bath Press, Avon

# Contents

# Introduction

JENNY WORMALD

Eleven years seem to have a particular significance in English history. In the seventeenth century, there were the eleven-year Personal Rule and the eleven-year Interregnum. In the twentieth, we have recently emerged from eleven years of Thatcher government. Apparently the English can stand just over a decade of constitutional shifts of rules and upheaval, and no more. Interregnum and Thatcherism (though not Personal Rule, which Charles I's northern kingdom did not experience) affected Scotland directly as both were imposed on England's junior partner, and both showed cracks in the union of the two countries, not least when they ended and the situation was rethought.

While Europe and the poll tax were issues trumpeted by the southern media as reasons for the downfall of Thatcher, the northern press can rightly add a third, the strains put on the union of England and Scotland by the intolerable experience of an English-elected government ruling a Scotland which rejected it, to the point where a fourth Thatcher election would almost certainly have reduced the already derisory number of Scottish Conservative members of Parliament to virtually none. One might say that the Scots have survived not the occasional eleven-year period of constitutional shifts, but to date 387 years, from the time when James I inherited the English throne in 1600, and in that much longer timespan gradually did settle into the role of junior and sometimes neglected partner. But the modern eleven years have produced a situation where Scotland's position within the United Kingdom can no longer automatically be taken for granted in the old way: if Thatcher forced questions about the nature of Britain's future place in Europe, she has also forced questions about the nature of Britain itself. Thus we have the paradox that the solidarity of one of the component parts of the wider political unit now being created is in itself in doubt. For the politician, Scotland is back on the agenda. For both politician and historian, therefore – and not just the historian of Scotland – Scotland, as a country with a long experience of being the lesser part of a wider unit, has something of crucial importance to offer, in the changing world of the 1990s. Yet its history is remarkably little known outside its own borders. The reason is understandable enough. But even in 'British' terms, it has lost its validity.

The professional study of history in Britain as in Europe developed in the nineteenth century, and English-speaking historians have tended to concentrate on states then formed or forming. Serious study takes its centre of gravity from London, as from Berlin, Rome or Madrid. To this extent, Scotland has been as ill-served as Bavaria, Naples or Catalonia; 'provinces' attracted interest (sometimes, as in the case of J.H. Elliott's work, in brilliant and illuminating ways) when they impinged on or resisted the centre, but rarely for their own sake and in their own right. In Scotland's case, the problem is compounded in two ways. First, the relevant state formation, the union of the crowns in 1603 and then the parliaments in 1707, occurred long before those of 'Germany' and 'Italy', the contemporary case studies for the state-centred historians of the nineteenth century. Second, English experience had already accustomed its historians – on both sides of the border – to think 'centrally' to a greater extent than those of any other country. Alexis de Tocqueville observed the 'pull' of Paris in his great work, *L'Ancien Régime et la Révolution*, as a factor highly relevant to his exploration of the ills within the French body politic, and not necessarily to be welcomed. English historians were far more inclined to take the 'pull' of London for granted. And not only historians.

In both perception and in reality, the northern and, until 1707, independent kingdom of Scotland became, as James VI and I had long ago forecast in 1607, 'as the northern shires, seldom seen and saluted by their king'. The intellectual stimulus provided by the luminaries of the Scottish Enlightenment and the vigour of the Scottish universities in the eighteenth century, in visible contrast to the torpor of eighteenth-century Oxbridge, the separate legal and educational systems, and above all the kirk, might all combine to remind the Scots of a separate identity, focused on their capital city of Edinburgh. But English preoccupations were quite different: the creation of an empire abroad and the maintenance of the perfect and balanced constitution at home. Aspiring Scotsmen left home, to make their mark in both worlds. For the 'North Britons', that was where the real opportunities were seen to lie.

And so there was created the ultimate paradox. The name 'Britain', loathed and rejected by the English when James VI and I tried to impose it on them after 1603, because they saw the disappearance of the proud name of England as a matter of profound humiliation, now became entirely acceptable. Sloppy conversationalists, at home and abroad, used it as interchangeable with England, and continue to do so. It was all made possible because Dr Johnson's 'noblest prospect that a Scotsman ever sees: the high road to England' became reality in the late eighteenth and nineteenth centuries. The nationalist writings of that most famous and popular novelist, Sir Walter Scott, were greeted with far more enthusiasm by nationalist movements in Europe than by his fellow Scots. It was certainly true that Scott and others of his circle did much to establish the basis for the academic history of Scotland, in the clubs they set up — Bannatyne, Maitland and others — to publish the sources of Scottish history; indeed, proportionately speaking, Scotland has an amazing quantity of historical records in print. But when they and their successors, men like Patrick Tytler and Robert Rait, wrote history themselves, they did so from an Anglo-centric viewpoint. They were following and confirming a trend begun in the seventeenth century, when James VI and I had tried to argue, to a hostile English parliament, that his Scottish subjects were a civilised people, with much in common with the English. Things Scottish which did not conform to English constitutional history were increasingly condemned; the myth of a weak Scottish parliament, the myth of excessive and barbarous violence in a country which did not enjoy the blessings of the great English legal system, born out of a desire for assimilation when the two kingdoms came together under a single king, grew apace in the hands of the historians of the nineteenth and early twentieth centuries.

But another problem bedevilled the study of Scottish history. Such has been the appeal of the greater rather than the lesser part of the British Isles that the best history graduates from the Scottish universities, carefully nurtured in their student days on a diet of what is euphemistically called 'British', but is actually 'English' history, also followed Johnson's 'high road to England' when it came to research; few resisted the lure. Scotland, as ancient and once as viable a historical entity as the kingdom of England, therefore became largely the preserve of the romantics. The 'history' of Scotland is too often colourful rather than intelligible, boiled down to a few events and personalities: the battles of Bannockburn,

Flodden, Solway Moss, Culloden, the massacre of Glencoe, the Darien disaster, William Wallace, Robert Bruce, John Knox and Bonnie Prince Charlie. It even features two horses, the first of which in the late fourteenth century kicked and lamed the future Robert III, thus reducing him to total rather than partial ineptitude, the second bearing the lamentable James III off the battlefield of Sauchieburn in 1488, a disgraced and cowardly king failing to fight his rebellious subjects. Above all, it features Mary Queen of Scots. But how many realise how intricately complicated, as well as desperately brave, was the political career of Robert Bruce, despite the magnificent study of him by G. W. S. Barrow? How many are aware of the reality which lies behind the romantic figure of the Highlander as invented by Walter Scott, who domesticated him, gave him his clan tartan and made him into a fashionable figure in the great Anglo-Scottish houses of nineteenth-century London? How many are aware that the independent kingdom of Scotland, small though it was, remote on the fringes of Europe, was far more European in its law, its political institutions and many of its customs, than its more powerful neighbour to the south, or that Scottish kings by their diplomacy and Scottish scholars and merchants by their presence in the greater European countries made an impact out of all proportion to the size and geographic position of the kingdom?

Between the popular landmarks of Scottish history there remain vast areas of darkness; it is extraordinary how little is yet known about Scotland, and therefore about an essential element in the formation of 'Great Britain'. But the historical experience of Scotland — small, impoverished, threatened before 1603 by aggressive annexation, and thereafter by peaceful assimilation and indifference, and yet a flourishing and successful society, influential enough to make itself noticed — is far more interesting than any amount of battles, romantic heroes or foolish queens. As Scotland made its mark on contemporaries, so its history deserves to make its mark on the historical world, for it offers insights into historical problems not necessarily illuminated by wealthier, more powerful, more centralised societies. For historians who prefer kings who signed their account books, such as Henry VII, and sophisticated and complex government institutions, such as the English parliament (even if, by the seventeenth century, its very complexity was in danger of making it unworkable), Scotland will always fall short. But these things were not necessarily the key to the success or failure, the political and social stability of medieval and early-modern kingdoms, or the yardstick by which contemporaries judged success; and a study of the history of Scotland does much to show why. Indeed, the outward-looking sturdy confidence of the Scots of the past provide the lineal ancestry for one notable success of the present: Glasgow was the European City of Culture in 1990.

In the second half of the twentieth century, thinking about the past began to change. The number of Scottish historians remains small. But they have started to approach their history, not as a pale reflection of the history of England, but in its own right and on its own terms. Monographs, articles and series such as the *Edinburgh History of Scotland* and the *New History of Scotland* all testify to the revolution in Scottish historical writing. Gloom and doom, 'thud and blunder', have gone. The replacement is infinitely more rewarding. And gradually it is attracting interest. Yet the junketing which surrounded the four-hundredth centenary of the execution of Mary Queen of Scots in 1987 shows that there is still a very long way to go before woolly romance gives way to a real understanding of Scotland's past, within and certainly outside Scotland. The magazine *History Today* has provided a welcome outlet for the new scholarship on Scotland in a series of articles concentrating on the early-modern period, that critical time of transition from being a whole to being a part. These articles seek to explain the nature and aspirations of what became England's junior partner. They thus elucidate not only the history of Scotland but the history of Britain. The articles are now reprinted here, with revisions and revised bibliographies. In this age, when a much greater assimilation than that of England and Scotland in 1603 is the burning and often agonising political issue, they may even serve as a reminder that becoming part of a wider whole may temporarily blur, but can never destroy, national identity.

# CHAPTER I

# The House of Stewart and its Realm

JENNY WORMALD

The house of Stewart began its career as the royal house of Scotland in 1371 with the accession of Robert II, namesake, grandson and dismal contrast to the great Robert Bruce. Its second representative, Robert III, is best remembered by his self-assessment 'the worst of kings and most miserable of men'. It wended its way down the line of 'the mournful procession of the five Jameses'; even the most attractive, James IV, stares vacantly out from his portrait in testimony to that characterisation. A misty aura of tedious romance hangs over it in the person of Mary Queen of Scots, although it derived heightened political interest from James VI who became James I of England, and Charles I whose head the English cut off. Only Charles II, whose interest in Scotland was minimal, was any fun; James VII and II, and his sad daughters Mary and Anne, rounded off this uninspiring collection of rulers, so lacking in colour compared with the great names of English and European kingship: Henry V, Henry VIII, Elizabeth, the Emperor Charles V, Philip II, François I, Henry IV, Louis XIV.

This admittedly oversimplified summary arises from a long historiographical tradition, whose keynote was not success, but failure and misfortune; the Stewarts were unlucky. It is also, of course, a travesty. Various elements have gone into its creation. First, the English tradition, with its heavy and often Whiggish emphasis on the constitution, set up a model for Scottish historians, who searched in vain for the same level of administrative and legal development in the government of Scotland, and, when they failed to find it, apologetically assumed that Scottish kingship must be both weak and underdeveloped; it does actually require a strenuous mental leap even for modern Scots, let alone anyone else, to recognise that the parliamentary and legal institutions of England are not essential prerequisites to the well-being of a kingdom.

Second, another and more general historical theme of the 'waning of the middle ages' is the conflict between kings and their greatest subjects, in a struggle for power which, by the early sixteenth century, was being resolved in favour of the monarchies. When examined in its Scottish context, this conflict looked stark and barbaric in its ferocity; if English and European rulers had problems, Scottish kings never slept easy in their beds at all, and of course rarely died there. Third, if the

*Embassy of Aeneas Sylvius Piccolomini, the future Pope
Pius II, to the court of King James I in 1428. A fresco by Pinturicchio.*

Scottish crown was associated with violence unleavened by concern with constitutional principles or indeed with the culture and civilisation of Renaissance Europe, it was also dramatised by romance. The comparative paucity of Scottish academic history left the field clear for excessive popularisation, not to say legend-peddling, exemplified in the obsessive interest in a few personalities, notably Mary Queen of Scots and Bonnie Prince Charlie: significantly, except for Robert Bruce, the historical failures.

This hybrid tradition may be linked to the crisis of identity ushered in by the removal of the Scottish monarchy to London in 1603, since when the incompatible appeals of 'Celt' and 'Saxon' have increasingly confused Scottish perception of the present and the past. A barrier to understanding was erected, which scholars are only now beginning to break down. For early-modern Scotland was very far from being the underdog of later centuries, with both the arrogance and the self-pity of that unfortunate brute; and Stewart kingship was anything but a failure. Scotland was certainly a poor country. Its kings did indeed lack the

13

machinery of government long established in precociously bureaucratic England and being built up in the major European kingdoms; and their revenue was by any standards derisory. Yet the authority of the crown, vested in the house of Stewart, was, despite the fates of three of the nine kings who reigned as kings of Scotland alone, never challenged; and most of the Stewart kings were men of terrifying power. Why?

The experience of the first two kings – dismissed in books and examination papers as the (Scottish) 'Early Stewarts', signifying the suitably anonymous introduction of this line of kings – immediately establishes a crucial clue. Both Robert II and Robert III visibly failed to rule. The problem in both cases was met by transferring executive power to the heir to the throne, even though the future Robert III was clearly more inept than his father, and David Duke of Rothesay, heir to Robert III, was something of a bully-boy with little political perception.

IACOBVS DEI GRATIA . SCOTOR. &c. REX .

*James II, 1430–60. James' facial disfigurement, which gave rise to his nickname 'James of the fiery face', can just be seen.*

At this point historical fact ends and the historians take over. Had this sort of crisis happened in late fourteenth-century England, a great deal of learned historical ink would have been spilled on a further chapter in the understanding of the 'constitution'. In Scotland, it has been seen only as evidence of the crude political dealings of the Scots and the weakness of their monarchy.

If the English model perhaps goes too far, the Scottish one does not go nearly far enough; for even if the Scots did not articulate a 'constitutional' point, they certainly got to the heart of the political matter: the fundamental importance of maintaining the authority of the monarchy when faced with the failure of the monarch. If late fourteenth-century Scotsmen did not get round to enunciating the theory of the King's Two Bodies, they were undoubtedly coming close to following it in practice. Their understanding of the nature of kingship, its political power and responsibilities, rested less on concern with the success or failure of individual kings than on a political instinct about kingship as the focal point which would hold together a fissiparous collection of highly localised communities.

This may appear to say very little. All kings had to preside over 'segmented' societies, and those who could draw on resources of wealth and government which far outstripped anything available to the Scottish crown would appear to have had a *prima facie* chance of greater success. A king who rules looks a better bet than a focal point. This is the great paradox of Scottish monarchy; out of its visible weaknesses came remarkable strengths. Even the most powerful of English or European monarchs never in fact had the resources, in men and money, to ensure their authority throughout their kingdoms; all were hedged about by the need to secure the co-operation of the leaders of the local communities. The more 'developed' kingdoms were therefore more vulnerable to the other aspect of crown-magnate relations – resistance.

In Scotland, where the crown did not attempt to impose its will on the localities to anything like the same extent, tension was correspondingly reduced, and such conflict as did arise was individual and personal rather than bound up in national politics. Scottish kings were never faced with the aristocratic coalitions of fifteenth-century France; there was nothing like the 'War of the Common Weal' in which a sizeable group of leading French magnates challenged Louis XI in the 1460s in defence of their collective rights. The one superficially similar Scottish coalition of the period, which defeated and killed James III in 1488, was not in any sense fighting for a collective aristocratic position or principle, but reacting to a series of provocative actions by a particular king against them as individuals. Only the Douglases, who rebelled against James II in the 1450s – again, initially, in response to arbitrary treatment – have anything in common with the rulers of the great French *apanages* in fighting for aris-

*J*ames III circa 1451–88. *Detail from an altarpiece by Van*
*der Goes.*

tocratic power as such: the difference was that they fought increasingly
alone, isolated from an aristocracy which would not line up against the
King. It is an instructive comparison. So also, perhaps, is a comparison
from a lower level on the social scale which again relates to the lack of
pressure put on its subjects generally by the Scottish crown: the absence
in Scotland of those outbreaks rightly or wrongly described as peasants'
revolts.

The reason is not that Scottish kings were more politically perceptive
than their contemporaries; and they were certainly not more pleasant
personalities. It lies in historical circumstances. There are superficial
similarities between the creations of the English and Scottish kingdoms

between the ninth and eleventh centuries. Otherwise, the contrast between their histories is stark. First, unlike England and France, Scotland was never a conquered country. Paradoxically, it is arguably easier to annex a country where there is a system of well-integrated local government, which has inculcated an awareness of public authority, and is there to be taken over. This was the case with Anglo-Saxon England; thus, despite its greater power and wealth, William the Conqueror met surprisingly little resistance, compared to the very different experience of Edward I when he moved against the less coherent kingdom of Scotland. Moreover, a foreign ruling élite had to bear more heavily on the localities as it established its control. Scotland, like England, was indeed 'Normanised', but by immigrants rather than conquerors; they assimilated rather than imposed, thus allowing the rulers of the Scottish kingdom to maintain a more *laissez-faire*, supervisory role.

Second, if Scotland was not a conquered country, neither was it a conquering one. Indeed, after the English imperialist dream fizzled out in the mid-fourteenth century, it was uniquely peaceful. The Scots went soldiering abroad, mainly in France – where they could bash the English enemy and pick up French money, lands, titles – but they showed extreme reluctance for 'national' warfare. Kings with a taste for it, like James III, who in the early 1470s wanted to cut a dash on the European scale by going conquering abroad, got short shrift from those whose consent was necessary. It cannot be overemphasised how much the disastrous battle of Flodden was a historical aberration. Far more typical was the refusal to rush to war even with the approach of an English army, in 1482 and 1542. Both these events resulted in Scottish humiliation. But the Scots could also humiliate; in 1400, the usurper Henry IV, seeking to boost his reputation at home by hammering the Scots, found himself trailing an English army round southern Scotland, meeting no Scottish army to fight, but only the heir to the throne, cheerfully greeting him from the secure heights of Edinburgh castle as he passed.

Such an attitude had a profound effect on the political balance at home. Warfare was immensely costly; the vast sums raised by the French and English governments came largely from regular taxation. That forced a reliance on, a need for consent by, the localities; hence the government's desire to sell its policies, the strong political involvement and response of the local communities, finding expression in local assembly and county court and, in England, the strident demands of the Commons in the national assembly for their right to consent to taxation. Hence also the need for an elaborate administrative machinery. In Scotland, lack of war meant lack of pressure on the localities. The Scottish parliament – the body which stopped James II in the 1470s – was strong and effective, and kings could not ignore it; it could concentrate on political realities, with less need to worry about constitutional principles. For honest Scotsmen, unlike their honest English counterparts, did not need to speak out in defence of their rights; a crown which simply did not impinge so much did not call these rights into being.

This did not mean that the Scots were denied national pride in their monarchy. The Stewart kings had no doubt of their European importance, even if their image was subjectively inflated. The two Roberts were the only kings to marry local girls; their successors moved in on the international marriage market. In the 1530s, James V married twice, first into the French royal house and second – beating no less a rival than Henry VIII, to his considerable fury – into the leading aristocratic house of Guise. James II thought himself important enough to act as arbiter between the French king and dauphin; James IV saw himself as uniting Christendom against the infidel Turk; James VI as the leader of Reformed Europe. Mary Queen of Scots inevitably let the side down, reducing her horizons from being Queen of France through marriage to François II, to being the wife successively of two Scots nobles, one – Darnley – wholly inept, the other – Bothwell – a political liability, and throwing away the intensely important European role which her nubility and her potential as a leading figure in the Counter-Reformation, as well as heir to the English throne, gave her. Her one contribution to the European vision of the Stewart monarchy was to change its name to the Frenchified 'Stuart'. Otherwise, every Stewart king ensured that a Europe which did not naturally think much about a small northern kingdom sat up and took notice. It was a remarkable achievement, and one which did much to strengthen the prestige of the crown at home. So also did their efforts to bring Europe to Scotland. Small-scale their palaces may have been, but splendid examples of northern European architecture they undoubtedly were; they housed courts in which foreign ambassadors and scholars met with native courtiers, musicians, poets, numerically small but culturally typical and sometimes brilliant examples of the early modern European court. And all this was achieved not by grandiose and costly military exploits, but by lofty self-opinion, shoestring diplomacy and an instinct for the right modes and fashions to follow.

Third, their most obvious apparent weakness, the lamentable habit of dying young leaving a minor to succeed, actually strengthened their curious political balancing act. That minorities were to be dreaded was almost a historical cliché. 'Woe unto thee, O land, when thy king is a child'; how could government function without major political disruption, when it was the king's government, given impetus and direction by him? The answer in Scotland was that it could function very well, for precisely the reasons outlined above; the comparatively high level of local autonomy under adult rulers meant that their temporary absence created little local disturbance. Perhaps even more important, the breaks caused

*J*ames IV, 1473–1513; Mytens portrait based on an earlier
drawing.

by minorities restrained the tendency towards an increasingly autocratic style of kingship, associated with the so-called 'new monarchies' of sixteenth-century France, Spain, England; every Scottish king, save Mary, showed signs of such a move, but none lived long enough nor left an heir old enough to bring it to fruition. Another crucial area of tension between governor and governed was thus rendered minimal. Instead, the repeated minorities offer further remarkable evidence of the nicely-poised relationship between the crown and its most powerful subjects. Every king from James II onwards issued an 'Act of Revocation', revoking grants made in his name during his minority; normally they were regranted, but not always – and sometimes for a price. In this age of 'over-mighty' aristocracies, the Scottish aristocracy accepted that gains made when the king was not personally in control should not be automatically permanent. It is a succinct comment on a political relationship of unusual stability.

This general situation was not, of course, without its individual crises and acts of violence; after all, only two of the seven monarchs who reigned between 1406 and 1625 – James V and James VI – died in their beds. James II was blown up by a cannon at the siege of Roxburgh, taken back from the English in 1460, and James IV was killed in battle against the English, at Flodden in 1513. But although Mary died by an English executioner's axe, she would hardly have found herself there had she not been forced to abdicate by a powerful faction of her Scottish subjects twenty years earlier; and James I and James III were killed by their subjects, the one assassinated in 1437, the other in the battle of Sauchieburn in 1488. There is indeed a distinction between Scottish kingship and individual Scottish kings. Leaving aside Mary, whose political folly was seemingly unlimited, they were all exceedingly

*W*ooden roundel from Stirling Castle, early sixteenth
century. Possibly a portrait of James V.

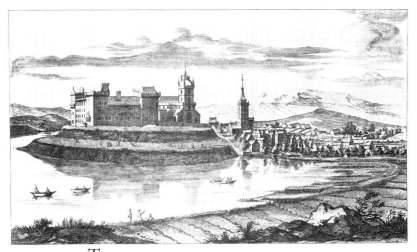

*The Palace of Linlithgow, one of the most magnificent of the Scottish palaces.*

able and tough, and (all but one) very grasping men; the one, James VI, cheerfully spent what his grasping predecessors had steadily acquired for the crown, but there is no doubt of his ability and toughness. There was no general conflict between crown and aristocracy, but there were conflicts between kings and magnates; as the vast Stewart kingroup found in James I's reign, the Douglases in James II's, and a string of other nobles in these and other reigns unwise enough to leave any legal chink in their landholding, the crown almost always won. On two occasions, it lost the last battle; James I was killed by a small group of members of his family, James III by a coalition of sufferers from twenty years of arbitrary rule in which his leading servants could never feel secure. But understanding of early-modern Scottish kingship has been distorted by concentration on these dramatic events. What should be emphasised is what these kings could get away with; in James III's case, it is the twenty years, and the fact that Sauchieburn only happened because the king broke two agreements with the opponents of his actions, which are the most important points.

Thus Scottish kingship is an example of an immensely resilient institution which triumphantly survived the occasional hiccoughs caused by the individuals who ran it. The interruption of adult and intelligent Stewart rule between James V's death in 1542 and James VI's personal government from the early 1580s – a period dominated by two minorities, the antics of Mary, and above all the Reformation – raises a mental block to the understanding of how successful the Stewart monarchy was. But it was not the weak king of a weak kingdom who came south in 1603; and looking back to the fifteenth century makes the picture much clearer.

21

Compare Scotland with England. In England, there were five violent changes of dynasty between 1399 and 1485, as well as the usurpation of Richard III in 1483. In Scotland, the violent destruction of two kings did not even threaten, let alone overthrow, the dynasty.

How important that was can be seen by another comparison, with the brilliant Burgundian state of the late fourteenth and fifteenth centuries – from which Scotland, like other European countries, drew in art, architecture, music. Burgundy, like Scotland, was a conglomeration of disparate areas, and its dukes, like Scottish kings, ruled over linguistically divided peoples; the 'official' languages were respectively French and Scots, but Philip the Good and Charles the Bold certainly spoke Flemish, while James IV apparently knew some Gaelic. Both were territories bordering on a greater power which looked on them with a predatory eye. Yet Scotland survived, Burgundy did not. The reason surely lies in the contrast between the Burgundian confederacy which being, in Maurice Keen's words, 'a series of contiguous lordships, brought together by dynastic diplomacy rather than true interest, could not coalesce to form the true semblance of a kingdom', and a series of contiguous lordships which *had* coalesced, under the strong and stable Scottish royal dynasty of the twelfth and thirteenth centuries, and remained a kingdom under the Stewart dynasty which had inherited the tradition of providing the *raison d'être* for their unity, and was never challenged. For reasons which may seem inexplicable to those who look for 'strong' central government, the interrupted Stewart kingship of the

'*M*emento Mori', panel of Mary Queen of Scots, 1542–87, painted on ridged board by an unknown artist.

loosely linked network of communities which made up their kingdom worked amazingly well; historians of more 'obvious' societies might ponder this.

James VI's departure for England in 1603 was not the most significant factor in changing the nature of Scottish kingship. Even before 1603, the balance between king and subjects was beginning to alter, partly because a spendthrift king introduced regular taxation for the first time ever; partly because the growing literacy of the leading laity brought them into royal government as professionals, ousting the professional cleric – whose services the Reformed Church in any case withdrew from the state; and partly because the courts of the kirk, from kirk session to general assembly, established a link between centre and locality closer than had ever existed before. Thus the localities were made forcibly aware of central government and its demands. Yet traditional attitudes to Scottish kingship were not at once disrupted. The old and the new came together to make absentee kingship, as exercised by James VI, a success; *laisser-faire* kingship, punctuated by minorities, provided long experience of managing without direct control from the top, and now that the 'minority' situation was permanent, the managing was done by leading politicians who had worked with the King in the 1590s and lived on throughout his English reign. Above all, the loss of the King was mitigated by Scottish pride in having reversed the process begun by that monster of Scottish tradition, Edward I, for it was *their* King who brought the kingdoms together; while in any case James continued to take a visible interest in his northern kingdom.

The dramatic change came with Charles I. Personally and politically, Charles was an English king, wholly out of sympathy with his northern subjects – as King James's old friends sadly and immediately realised – and at the same time a man of considerable energy and determination to impose his rule. If the localities in the late sixteenth century had been wakened from the slumbers of relative autonomy, the whole kingdom in the mid-seventeenth was abruptly shaken out of its complacent experience of a kingship which had sat lightly. The religious susceptibilities of a people who believed that theirs was the purest of reformed kirks were violently threatened; so also was the political framework of the state. It is almost symbolic that Charles I should issue an Act of Revocation as his predecessors had done – with this vast difference, that he had not had a minority and he revoked grants made not just in his lifetime but going back to 1542.

However good his intentions – and in part, at least, the Act was designed to provide a sound financial basis for the kirk – this was not kingship as the Scots understood it. The combination of royal indifference and royal interference, both displayed at an intolerable level, has much to do with the fact that the 'Great Rebellion' broke out in Scot-

*James VI and his Lennox cousins praying at Darnley's cenotaph, 1567.*

land; the English Civil War might never have happened had it not been for the Scottish revolt, and to that extent the abuse, in Scottish eyes, of the exercise of Scottish kingship has an exceedingly important place in the history of Britain. Yet the past was not eradicated even by the activities of this king; the old belief in paternalistic kingship – *rex Scottorum*, not *rex Scotiae* – was still alive when, in 1649, the English executed Charles I and forcibly reminded them of their very personal, even proprietary affection for *their* monarchy – resulting in their last vigorous response, as a kingdom, to the actions of an English government, and, as so often before, to ruinous defeat at the battle of Dunbar (1650) and the battle of Worcester (1651).

And that in a sense is the end of the story. Thereafter the history of Scottish kingship is really the history of English kingship, with the Scots themselves torn between their traditional attitudes and the new realisation that, even if they could maintain their separate political, legal and religious identity – as they emphatically did when the union of the parliaments came in 1707 – the centre of their political world was London, not Edinburgh. It was not an easy transition for all, as the strength of Jacobitism and the lingering loyalty to the Stewart line showed; it was a necessary one, as the successful eighteenth-century political leaders, the 'North Britons', demonstrated. The gates of Traquair House in the Borders and, more curiously, of Trinity College, Oxford, both closed until the return of the Stewarts, show how far, since the seventeenth century, romance has taken over from history, even in the most unlikely places. But romance has obscured, and historians underrated, the historical importance of the Stewart kings of independent Scotland and at least the first Stewart king of Britain.

# CHAPTER II

# The Kingship of James IV of Scotland: 'The Glory of All Princely Governing'?

NORMAN MACDOUGALL

Even if we take into account the tendency towards exaggeration of most, if not all, sixteenth-century Scottish writers, Sir David Lindsay's famous epithet about James IV appears more than fulsome in its praise of the ruler of a small, geographically remote, and economically poor European country. Obviously James IV cannot be compared in terms of power, wealth, and international importance with his contemporaries, Henry VII and Henry VIII of England, the Emperor Maximilian, or Louis XII of France. But Lindsay was writing in 1530, at the end of the longest and most factious royal minority in medieval Scottish history, and therefore at a time when the relatively well-ordered and peaceful years of James IV's reign – the period of Lindsay's own youth – must have seemed like a distant golden age, lost for ever on one ghastly afternoon at Flodden. We may therefore allow Lindsay some poetic licence, the more so as his view of King James echoes those of contemporaries who knew the King well; and James IV's reputation as an outstanding ruler has stood the test of time, for he is widely regarded in our own time as a paragon amongst medieval Scottish kings.

It may be, however, that James IV's reputation has been artificially enhanced by contrasting him to his advantage with his immediate predecessors, above all with his father James III. This enigmatic ruler had some statesmanlike ideas – for example his 1474 alliance with England anticipates by a generation the Treaty of Perpetual Peace of 1502 for which James IV is now universally praised – but these qualities were more than offset by the negative aspects of his personality. Shifty and aloof, rarely moving from his favourite burgh of Edinburgh in the course of two decades, James III had a dangerously exalted concept of Stewart kingship, and totally failed to realise that he must reward support as well as punish rebellion. His arbitrary – and on occasions illegal – distribution of patronage, together with his appalling treatment of his brothers and sisters, led to a major Stewart rebellion in 1482 which he survived without learning wisdom from the experience.

Then, in 1488, James went too far, simultaneously outlawing the powerful border family of Hume and threatening any magnates who might side with them, alienating and then sacking his Chancellor, Colin

Campbell, Earl of Argyll, a loyal servant of the crown for more than a quarter of a century, and conferring honours on his *second* son, creating fears that he intended to cut his son and heir, James, Duke of Rothesay (the future James IV) out of the succession. The result was a civil war in which all those with grievances against James III sided with the young heir to the throne, while many potential supporters of the crown, alienated by King James' aggressiveness, ineptitude, and public breaches of faith, stood apart from the struggle and let the rebels win. The end came at Sauchieburn near Stirling on June 11th, 1488, in a battle fought more or less on the site of Bruce's great victory at Bannockburn in 1314. Displaying a sense of history rather than common sense, King James went into battle bearing Bruce's sword, and was killed on or near the field.

James III had been an unsatisfactory and overbearing ruler; but his death in battle against his own subjects led by his son was an event without parallel in medieval Scottish history. Much has been made of James IV's penance for his part in an act of patricide and regicide; certainly his outward display of repentance was impressive, and the famous penitential iron belt which he wore next to his skin was no myth invented by later chroniclers. It is however unlikely that the new King, aged fifteen on his accession, shed many tears for his father. Although he had given orders before the battle that no one should lay violent hands on James III, once the deed was done he was swift to take advantage of it, as he is to be found issuing a charter as James IV on the day after Sauchieburn. He had small cause to love – and perhaps little opportunity to know – his father, for he had been brought up at Stirling in the care of his mother, Margaret of Denmark, who had become estranged from James III during the rebellion of 1482, and who probably saw her husband only very rarely thereafter before her death in July 1486. Thus at the impressionable age of thirteen, Prince James had not only been deprived of his mother's counsel but was also slighted by his father, who seems to have reduced the Prince's household allowance and preferred his younger brother – significantly also named James – in his projected English marriage schemes of 1486 and 1487. In the circumstances, the young heir to the throne probably needed little persuading to throw in his lot with the rebels in February 1488; and once he had become King as James IV, he indicated his respect for his mother by at once endowing masses for Margaret of Denmark's soul. He would not do the same for his father for another eight years.

In the summer of 1488, the first concern of the new regime was survival at home, closely followed by the need for recognition abroad. Within Scotland itself, it was impossible to disguise the fact that the lion's share of royal patronage had gone to the most prominent rebels – the Earl of Argyll, at once restored as Chancellor, the powerful southern family of Hume, and – perhaps above all – the Hepburns, headed by Patrick, Lord Hailes, immediately created Earl of Bothwell, and his formidable uncle John, prior of St Andrews, the new Privy Seal. These men dominated – and would continue to dominate – the government. But their near-monopoly of power provoked widespread resentment, and much of 1489 was spent in quelling a rebellion which involved a combination of disappointed office-seekers in the south and west, and supporters of the late King in the north-east. In January of 1489, the Master of Huntly wrote to Henry VII of England, complaining that no punishment had been meted out to the slayers of James III, and condemning usurpation in very general terms; but these were pleas hardly calculated to win the support of the first Tudor king.

For all that, the rebellion was an extremely serious challenge to the new Scottish government. In the west of Scotland, the Earl of Lennox, his son Matthew and Lord Lyle garrisoned the castles of Crookston, Duchal, and Dumbarton, and issued an elaborate apologia explaining their actions as loyal supporters of the late King who resented his killing by vile and obscure persons, and the misappropriation of his treasure.

*William Elphinstone, Bishop of Aberdeen, Chancellor of Scotland, Privy Seal and founder of the University of Aberdeen.*

The crisis came when the north-eastern forces of the Master of Huntly and his allies joined up with the Lennox rebels in Dumbarton, and in October, in a frightening reminder of 1488, made a bid to seize James IV at Stirling. The new King's first experience of warfare, therefore, came within a year of his accession. On October 11th, 1489, the rebels were defeated at Gartloaning, and the royal forces were able to lay siege to Dumbarton itself. The rising was over before the end of the year, and King James' advisers had the good sense to annul the forfeitures already passed against Lennox, his son and Lyle. Thereafter moderation and conciliation were features of government policy. Already parliament had accepted that James III 'happened to be slain' at Sauchieburn; in 1492 the estates offered a reward – never claimed – for the apprehension of his killers. Furthermore, the 1488 rebels' tight control of offices in state and household was to some extent modified by bringing back on to the council former supporters of James III, men like David Lindsay, Earl of Crawford, William Scheves, Archbishop of St Andrews, and William Elphinstone, Bishop of Aberdeen.

Elphinstone's rapid acceptance by the new regime is perhaps the most striking example of its moderation. Although he had served James III for many years, rising to become Chancellor in the last few months of the reign, he was soon to be found taking an active part in the government of James IV; and his tenure of the office of Privy Seal, an unbroken twenty-two years from 1492, is a measure of the trust accorded him by the new King. It was however a trust which the Bishop had to earn, not only by trekking abroad in the first of many efforts to find a suitable bride for King James, but also by endorsing the new regime's written vindication of its actions at Sauchieburn, copies of which were to be sent to the Pope, and to the Kings of France, Spain and Denmark. In fact, tales about James III, which provide a lurid contrast with the sober official account of 1488 furnished by the Scots, were already circulating in Europe. In Denmark it was said that John Ramsay, the late King's favourite, had poisoned Margaret of Denmark in 1486; in France James III was held directly responsible for the murder of his brother, the Earl of Mar; and in the Empire it was even rumoured that King James, emulating Caligula, had had two children by his younger sister Margaret. Much nearer home, the most obvious threat to the Scottish revolutionaries of 1488, Henry VII of England, merely tested the strength of the new government with a few abortive schemes involving the Scottish 'fifth column', James III's uncle, the Earl of Buchan, his familiar John Ramsay and his lord advocate John Ross of Montgrenan. These schemes received little or no support, and in time all three men were pardoned and readmitted to James IV's court and council.

Thus within seven years of his accession, King James had quelled the only opposition to his kingship within Scotland, his regime was recognised by foreign rulers and the papacy, and he took personal control of government in 1495 after the shortest royal minority of the century. In some ways his experience was similar to that of Edward III of England in the early fourteenth century; like Edward, James was a young man succeeding to the throne following a palace revolution which had resulted in the death of his father, and entering on his inheritance with the assistance of a sizeable party of magnates who had suffered during the previous reign. This was an advantage in the sense that James IV enjoyed wide support from the outset of his personal rule, and indeed had little trouble with any of the Scottish nobles throughout the reign; but the price he had to pay to retain this support was a policy of appeasement towards his greatest subjects, Hume and Hepburn in the south, Argyll and Huntly in the west and north. Latterly even Matthew Stewart, Earl of Lennox, a rebel in 1489, was admitted to the royal council and became a regular charter witness. Thus, as Dr Trevor Chalmers has convincingly shown, by the end of James IV's reign the council displayed a much broader territorial representation than had ever been known under his three predecessors; more than that, the great families were now regularly involved in the business of royal government and administration. The contrast with James III and his familiars – Scheves, Ramsay, Ross, Carlyle and the rest – could not have been greater.

Undoubtedly, therefore, James IV's government was popular in the sense that – uniquely in the late medieval period – the royal council was truly representative of the most powerful men in the kingdom, which in turn meant that, in theory at least, every subject of the crown might find a patron at court. Yet it is extremely doubtful whether this change may be interpreted, to cite Dr Nicholson's phrase, as 'New Monarchy Triumphant'. Really James IV had little or no choice in his distribution of rewards, and even a cursory glance at the five major beneficiaries of royal patronage after 1488 – Hume, Hepburn, Argyll, Angus and Huntly – soon reveals that four of them were rebels whom the new King had to favour, while the fifth, George Gordon, second Earl of Huntly, had practised a studied neutrality in the latter stages of the civil war of 1488, thereby abandoning James III to his fate. Thereafter for the first time in the history of the Gordon family, Huntly looked for rewards not only in further extension of his estates in the north-east, but also in the acquisition of high office in central government. He was Chancellor from 1497 until his death in 1501; and his son Alexander, third Earl (and, as Master of Huntly, a former rebel of 1489), was by far the most powerful magnate in northern Scotland in the last years of the reign. Even the most notorious troublemaker of the previous reign, Archibald, Earl of Angus, showed little sign of being a reformed character after 1488; for he soon entered into treasonable dealings with Henry VII of England, and there followed a royal siege of his castle of

*J*ames IV and his Queen Margaret, the eldest daughter of
Henry VII of England. From the Seton
Armorial circa 1600.

Tantallon in October 1491; yet a year later, when his niece Marion
Boyd had become James IV's mistress, Angus was made Chancellor,
and by 1498 he was sharing another mistress, Janet Kennedy, with the
King. This is surely royal appeasement and reconciliation carried to its
utmost limits.

It may of course be argued that no other behaviour was possible
for a late medieval Scottish king if he wished to achieve a measure of
success and popularity. In a kingdom where, in the words of Dr Ronald
Cant, the king's function was to regulate rather than to rule, where there
was no tradition of regular taxation, where the king could not afford a
mercenary army to overawe his subjects, the only way in which he could
properly perform his main functions as lawgiver and leader in war was
to delegate authority widely to trustworthy magnates in the localities.
To a greater or lesser extent, the first three Jameses had accepted this
principle of delegation; but in an effort to increase their authority and
resources, they had also adopted ruthlessly aggressive attitudes towards

their more powerful subjects, especially the great Stewart and Black Douglas kingroups. James IV had no need to be aggressive towards the higher nobility; and wisely, he did not try to be.

Thus with the exceptions of two early aberrations – the rising of 1489 and Angus's machinations in 1491 – the reign of James IV provides us with the remarkable spectacle of king and nobility at peace for a quarter of a century. King James busied himself with the task of enforcing the law, making his presence felt in a way that his father had never done by hurrying about the country on justice ayres, displaying a conventional piety by regular pilgrimages to the shrines of St Duthac at Tain and St Ninian at Whithorn, and earning an impressive reputation for his athletic prowess. 'In manliness in jousting or fighting, either on foot or horseback', remarked Adam Abell a generation later, 'he had few like him in Scotland of his stature.' As an Observantine friar, Abell was of course biased in James IV's favour, for the King had been generous to his order; the Stirling friary, a James IV foundation much frequented by the King in Easter week, was an Observantine house, as was the beautiful little church of Ladykirk on the River Tweed near Coldstream, traditionally founded by King James in thanksgiving for his narrow escape from drowning in the river in 1497. Abell's praise of the King's jousting ability is reflected in contemporary evidence relating to tournaments at Edinburgh and Stirling, above all the great three-day-long Holyrood tournament of May 1508 in which James IV entertained champions from England, France and Denmark, attired himself in black and overcame all opponents in defence of the 'black lady', a negress imported for the occasion, possibly the 'lady with the meikle lippis' referred to by the poet Dunbar.

Athletic, warlike and pious, James IV may well be regarded as the ideal medieval king. He was also praised for his liberality, which raises the question of the amount available to him to spend. In an average year in the early 1500s, the total royal revenue from all regular sources – crown lands, customs, profits of justice, and so on – amounted to perhaps £30,000 Scots (that is, about £7,500 sterling). If the King's prodigality – and the increasing cost of royal administration – was to be afforded, more money had to be found without regular recourse to taxation. It was found, as Dr Nicholson has convincingly demonstrated, by more efficient exploitation of crown lands – above all by setting royal lands in feu-farm in the later years of the reign – by extracting money from debtors by 'apprising' (that is, valuing lands for sale to pay off debts), by recovering through 'recognition' – that is, repossession – lands which had been improperly alienated, and by exacting fees and fines for royal charters of confirmation of landholding.

On the strength of this high-powered activity to make money for the crown, Nicholson claims that 'the rosy picture of an easy-going

King is hardly credible'; and it is certainly true that the contemporary poets Dunbar and Henryson condemned the practice of feu-farming on the grounds that poor tenants could not afford the new and higher feu-duties and were therefore easily evicted, while no less than five sixteenth-century chroniclers attacked frequent royal use of recognition. The King managed to duck much of the unpopularity associated with these measures, and he could in any case afford to be unconcerned; for the money or lands acquired by the crown in these ways gave him a great ability to reward men on whose loyalty he relied, men like the Hepburns, Huntly and Lennox. If the magnates were satisfied with their King, what did the plight of the poor tenants of the earldom of March – rapidly converted to feu-farm in January 1510 – really matter? James IV might make the occasional gesture in the direction of John the Commonweel – as when he gave fourteen shillings to a poor man sitting at the road-side beside his dead horse – but this is hardly to be compared with his expenditure on royal artillery or the navy, or his extensive distribution of wealth and honours amongst powerful members of the nobility and royal familiars.

The members of this latter group were not condemned as James III's familiars had been, mainly because they never acquired a dominant role in framing royal policy. They included household knights like Sir Alexander McCulloch of Myreton, wealthy burgesses like Alexander Lauder, provost of Edinburgh, and favoured seamen like Sir Andrew Wood. The most bizarre was undoubtedly John Damian, an Italian (or possibly Frenchman) who captured James IV's interest around 1502 by claiming to be an alchemist. The King gave him money for over ten years to carry on experiments to discover the elixir of life, and even granted him the commend of the Abbey of Tongland for a time. However, Damian's search for the quintessence, which required regular supplies of *aqua vitae*, may have done little more than induce drunkenness; and he may have been in an advanced state of intoxication when, in September 1507, he attempted to fly with home-made wings from the battlements of Stirling castle to Paris, plummeted into a midden and broke his thigh-bone, to the delight of the poet William Dunbar, whose two satires on Damian barely conceal the sour grapes of the disappointed office seeker. But Dunbar at least retained his royal pension, generously increased as the reign went on; the wretched Damian, shorn of his commend of Tongland, last appears in the records in the spring of 1513, trying to make money out of the gold mines on Crawford Moor – an appropriate end for a failed alchemist. In the course of a decade, Damian's experiments cost King James a few hundred pounds; and it is unlikely that the alchemist caused more offence at court – except to William Dunbar – than the fiddler to whom the King paid fourteen shillings to play all night outside his lodgings in Crail.

If Damian's pension was a mere drop in the bucket, on what did James IV spend his money? A great deal of ink has been spilled over his expenditure on architecture; and it is true that he spent many thousands on Holyrood palace, on a royal hall at Edinburgh castle and on the chapel royal and great hall at Stirling castle (the last persistently and erroneously attributed by many modern writers to James III). But others found similar sums of money for new educational establishments – Aberdeen University, the brainchild of Bishop Elphinstone, founded in 1495, and St Leonard's College at St Andrews University, founded jointly by Archbishop Alexander Stewart (James IV's bastard son) and Prior John Hepburn in 1512. The King's interest in these foundations, and indeed in education in Scotland as a whole, may not have gone very deep. After all, James sent his two illegitimate sons abroad to be educated, and, in spite of the claims of the flattering Spanish ambassador Pedro de Ayala about royal proficiency in seven languages, the King himself is to be found in 1506 paying large sums to a shrewd expatriate Scot in the Low Countries, James Inglis, for some books on alchemy written *in English*.

In fact, contemporary records leave us in no doubt that James IV considered himself first and foremost a warrior. His expenditure on warfare by land and sea, that is on artillery and a navy, is remarkable by any standards, and quite astonishing for the ruler of a small and remote European kingdom. Over the entire period of the reign, the cost of buying, building, outfitting and maintaining a Scottish navy, and paying the crews to man it, cannot have come to less than £100,000 Scots – and it may have totalled substantially more. The showpiece of the fleet, the 'great' *Michael*, an enormous capital ship with a crew of 300, costing over £30,000 and launched in 1511, was immediately copied by the young Henry VIII of England (a man whose warlike delusions of grandeur were matched only by his blindness to the realities of European politics), who built the *Henri Grace à Dieu* to more or less the same specifications in 1512. King James loved the *Michael*; he brought tapestries from Falkland to hang on her walls when he dined on board; he allotted some of his best foreign gunners to her crew; and, on wages alone, about one-tenth of his annual income would be required to maintain a full crew on this one ship. Perhaps for this reason, the *Michael*'s career in Scots service was brief, for after Flodden she was sold to Louis XII of France and absorbed into the French navy as *La Grande Nef d'Ecosse*.

Hardly less impressive was royal expenditure on artillery. James IV inherited from his grandfather the largest cannon in Britain, Mons Meg, and for appearances' sake had this enormous weapon trundled back and forth to – or at least in the direction of – the sieges of Duchal in 1489 and Norham in 1497. Apart from this monster, the King had to pay for the making of guns at Stirling and Edinburgh –

'bombards' or siege guns, field guns of smaller calibre, and hand-guns – and a huge army of specialists and labourers to build, maintain and fire the artillery, and above all convey the guns to the places of siege. All of James' expeditions – to Crookston, Duchal and Dumbarton in 1489, Tantallon in 1491, Heton in 1496, Norham in 1497, and Norham, Etal and Ford in 1513 – involved vast royal expenditure on artillery.

To this formidable combination of a co-operative nobility and a huge arsenal of up-to-date weaponry may be added James IV's growing confidence in himself as a European ruler of major importance. From the turn of the century, we may detect King James's personal interest in internal Scottish problems diminishing; for example, his last visit to the Highland west was in 1498, and then he went no further than Kilkerran castle, his newly built stronghold in Kintyre. The 'daunting' of troublemakers in the Highlands and Islands was largely left to his lieutenants Argyll and Huntly; for the King had evolved a considerable interest in foreign ventures. These included a naval expedition to assist his kinsman King Hans of Denmark against the rebellious Swedes in 1502; the construction, from the winter of the same year, of a navy with French assistance for 'the defence of Scotland', as the King put it, though his purpose seems to have been offensive rather than defensive; and by the last years of the reign, King James had become totally preoccupied with efforts to build a European alliance consisting of Denmark, France, Scotland, Gueldres and a number of Irish princes to counter the cynical 'Holy League' directed against Louis XII of France by Pope Julius II. James' young and aggressive brother-in-law Henry VIII of England planned to use the League to further his totally unrealistic dreams of conquests in France on a scale comparable with those of Edward III and Henry V. Thus in 1513 the brittle Anglo-Scottish Treaty of Perpetual Peace of 1502 finally snapped, and James IV, having sent his fleet to France, invaded Northumberland with a huge army to support his ally Louis XII in a European war.

His objective was Norham castle, the great stronghold of the Bishop of Durham just south of the River Tweed, a target for the Scots for the past fifty years. At the end of August it was taken by storm after a week's siege; but less than a fortnight later, the King's initially successful raid ended in total disaster at Flodden, when in a few hours of wind and rain on the late afternoon of September 9th, 1513, the English commander, the aged Earl of Surrey, outmanoeuvred and outfought the Scots. King James, with his artillery hopelessly misplaced, was probably killed early in the battle, and in the carnage that followed virtually the entire Scottish political community was wiped out – the royal bastard Alexander, Archbishop of St Andrews, one bishop, two abbots, nine earls, fourteen lords of parliament, and thousands of rank and file. Of the great lords, Huntly, Angus and Hume survived. Angus, who had

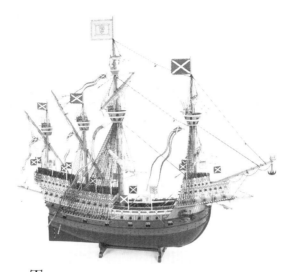

*T*he Great Michael, *a model of James IV's warship which was completed in 1511 at a cost of over £30,000.*

sent his two sons to be killed in the battle, died two months later and was succeeded by his irresponsible grandson, whose subsequent antics brought ruin to his family within a generation. Hume was executed for treason only three years later; and even Bishop Elphinstone of Aberdeen, the most outstanding ecclesiastical statesman of his day, did not long survive the Flodden disaster, being nominated as Archbishop of St Andrews only in 1514, the year of his death.

In political terms, therefore, Flodden marks the end of an era, for the government of the infant James V inevitably fell prey to the intrigues of those who supported the English queen-mother or the French governor, John, Duke of Albany. Thus the reign of James IV may be seen in retrospect as perhaps the only period during which the delicately balanced crown-magnate relationship which was the ideal of Stewart monarchy, the *'laissez-faire'* monarchy described by Dr Jenny Wormald, really worked smoothly; and it is at once fitting and ironic that the same classes as had refused to support the unpopular James III's grandiose continental schemes in 1473 should have paid with their lives for becoming involved in those of his popular son. For James IV's first serious – and in the event fatal – mistake was made on the last day of his life, when he committed himself to battle with the Earl of Surrey; and this was the product of over-confidence. The leaders of the Scottish host should have been warned by that unwitting Cassandra, Don Pedro de Ayala, who as early as 1498 had summed up James IV's greatest strength *and* principal failing in a sentence. 'He esteems himself', remarked Ayala, 'as much as though he were lord of the world'.

# CHAPTER III

# The Court as a Cultural Centre

RODERICK LYALL

In March 1504, the Treasurer to James IV of Scotland recorded a payment from the royal purse as an offering at the first Mass of a royal servant, the poet William Dunbar. The relationship between the verse of Dunbar and life at his master's court is unusually close and remarkably explicit, whether he is petitioning for financial support:

> I haif inquyrit in mony a place
> For help and confort in this cace,
>    And all men sayis, my lord, that ye
> Can best remeid for this malice
> That with sic panis prickillis me,

or offering carefully-worded advice on the occasion of the King's impending marriage to the fourteen-year-old Margaret of England:

> And sen thow art a king, thow be discreit;
> Herb without vertew thow hald nocht of sic pryce
> As herb of vertew and odor sueit;
> And lat no nettill vyle and full of vyce
> Hir fallow to (*associate with*) the gudly flour delyce,
> Nor latt no wyld weid full of churlichenes
> Compair hir till the lilleis nobilnes,

or engaging in boisterous self-caricature as he celebrates 'ane dance in the Quenis chalmer':

> Than cam in Dunbar the mackar (*poet*),
> On all the flure thair was nane frackar (*readier*),
> and thair he dancet the dirrye dantoun;
> He hoppet lyk a pillie wanton
>    For luff of Musgraeffe, men tellis me;
> He trippet quhill he tint his panton: (*till he lost his slipper*)
>    A mirrear dance mycht na man see.

The participants in this last occasion, from Mrs Musgrave to Sir John Sinclair ('new cum owt of France') and Mr Robert Shaw, are all referred to in the accounts of the royal household; and it is evident that Dunbar was writing in this familiar, comic vein to entertain the court.

*J*ester at the court of James V. A wooden roundel from the
ceiling of the Presence Chamber of Stirling Castle.

The household of a medieval king was an intimate, enclosed society, and Dunbar is not unusual among Scottish poets in the respectful familiarity with which he treats the King and Queen. Nor does his dependence upon their patronage mark him off from other writers in Middle Scots, even if the court milieu plays a more prominent part in his poetry than is generally the case. There is reason to believe, indeed, that it was royal patronage which was responsible for the emergence of later medieval Scots verse as we now know it.

John Barbour, whose *Brus* (written *circa* 1375–76) celebrates the life and deeds of Robert I, was a royal servant under his hero's grandson Robert II (1371–90), and he received a pension from 1378 which was believed by fifteenth-century administrators to have been granted 'for the writings of the book of the deeds of the late King Robert the Bruce'. It is likely that Barbour's early ecclesiastical preferment, first as precentor of Dunkeld and then as Archdeacon of Aberdeen, came with support from Robert Stewart, the Governor of Scotland who later succeeded as Robert II; and both the *Brus* itself and the lost genealogy of the Stewarts, which is attributed to Barbour, indicate that he was in some measure a propagandist for the newly established Stewart dynasty. The *Brus* is the earliest extant work in Scots, a long romance in octosyllabic verse which rejoices in the feats of both Robert I and his faithful lieutenant James Douglas, giving an inspiring portrait of feudal lordship in a time of profound national crisis. It is difficult to resist the idea that the story of the Scots' successful resistance against Edward I and Edward II, the moral basis of which is carefully pointed out by Barbour, was intended to provide a model for the new King and his magnates.

The bitter struggle for independence at the beginning of the four-teenth century had clearly made a lasting impression on the Scots, and the periodic recurrence of the conflict kept the issue of national identity alive in men's minds. The sense of distinctiveness which the Scots had developed as a result, which is well embodied in the national myth of the origin of the Scottish kings in the union of the Greek prince Gathelos with Scota, the daughter of Pharaoh, may indeed have fostered the creation of a vernacular literature in Scots, and the earliest writers to follow Barbour's example, such as the anonymous author of the Scottish saints' lives and the chronicler Andrew Wyntoun, include a proportion of patriotic material in their works. Wyntoun, a canon of the Augustinian priory of St Andrews and the prior of its daughter-house at Loch Leven, sets the history of Scotland within the framework of a world-history drawn from biblical and continental monastic sources, doing so as he tells us:

> . . .at be instance of ane larde
> That has my seruice in his warde,
> Schir Johne of Wemys be rycht name,
> A worthy knycht and of gud fame,
> Albeid his lordschip be nocht like
> To gretare lordis in be kinrik.

This acknowledgement serves to remind us that the royal court was not the only possible source of patronage in medieval Scotland, and there is some evidence that a number of magnates and lairds also had literary interests. Sir Gilbert Haye, a former member of the household of Charles VII of France, was commissioned both by William Sinclair, Earl of Orkney and by Robert, Lord Erskine to translate French chivalric and military works into Scots prose or verse after his return to his native land during the reign of James II.

The influence of the Sinclair family was clearly considerable, not only through the commissioning of such works as Haye's prose translations and Gavin Douglas' translation of the *Aeneid*, which was occasioned by

Orkney's grandson Henry, Lord Sinclair, but also through the acquisition of manuscripts. In particular, it is to Lord Sinclair that we owe the survival of the *Kingis Quair*, a poem which was apparently conceived in the English court during the captivity of James I, but which now exists in a single manuscript, a Chaucerian miscellany of English and Scottish poems written, it would seem, for Sinclair in the first years of the reign of James IV. It may be, indeed, that the occasion for the gathering together for this collection of love poems was the marriage of Lord Sinclair to Margaret Hepburn, which took place some time before December 4th, 1489. If, as seems most likely, the *Kingis Quair* was indeed composed by James I about the time of his own marriage to Joan Beaufort in 1424, it represents a new departure in Scots verse, breaking with the tradition of octosyllabic couplets and introducing an elegant style of allegorical poetry modelled on the work of the English court poets Chaucer, Gower and Lydgate. It was a style which dominated the court cultures of every nation in Western Europe, and there is ample evidence that James was not without his imitators in Scotland.

The entertainment of the royal court, or of the households of the magnates, was no doubt an important consideration in the composition of many Middle Scots literary works. But entertainment was very often mingled with instruction, and there are numerous examples of poets exercising the function of licensed adviser. One of the most clear-cut (as well as being among the earliest) is the anonymous *Buke of Gud Counsale*, a poem incorporated into the chronicle known as the *Liber Pluscardensis*, and which deals with the reign of James II. It was written, moreover, in response to a royal commission.

> My soverane Lord, sen thow hes gevin me leif,
> To fynd faltis that forfaltis to thy croun,
> Quhilkis (*which*) to thi majestie may gane stand or greve . . .

The prevailing themes are traditional: the need for reform in the administration of justice, the danger to the kingdom from grasping counsellors, and the prevalence of corruption. But there is also a specific reference to the financial problems of the crown, in terms which leave little doubt that the poem was written shortly after James took over the reins of government in 1449. The political commonplaces take on a new sharpness if they are related to the crisis years 1449–52:

> this may thow se suth be experience,
> Be officiaris that has thi gude to spend:
> Thai ger (*cause*) the trow thou may nocht mak dispense
> On thin housald, nocht half a yeir til end;
> But in hunting and in sornying thai the send
> On lordis and on abbayis heir and thair –
> Thai by lordschippis, bot thou art alway bair.

On this interpretation, we should see the *Buke of Gud Counsale* not as a disinterested piece of political advice, but as a propagandist work, part of a factional struggle within the government. That the role of courtier-poet might draw a writer into such a position should not surprise us, for the line between the court as a cultural meeting-place and the royal household as a centre of political intrigue can seldom have been a very clear one.

Another view of the crisis which followed James II's assumption of personal power is offered by the *Buke of the Howlat*, a poem in alliterative stanzas composed by Richard Holland for Elizabeth Dunbar, Countess of Moray and her husband Archibald Douglas at their castle at Darnaway. There could not be a greater contrast with the *Buke of Gud Counsale*. The latter is rhetorically simple, no more than a series of injunctions, whereas the *Buke of the Howlat* is so complex an amalgam of poetic conceits that its coherence is at times in question. Its central figure is the Howlat (or owl) himself, so unhappy with his ugly appearance that he appeals to the Pope and the Emperor and is eventually taken pity on by Nature, who provides him with a feathered cloak made up of one feather from each of the other birds. He instantly becomes so arrogant that Nature revokes her edict, and the Howlat is left to lament his folly and the uncertainty of the things of this world:

> Now mark you mirour be me, all maner of mar
> Ye princes, prentis (*images*) of pryde for penneis and prowe,
>> That pullis the pure ay,
>> (*who constantly harass the poor*)
>> Ye sall syng as I say:
>> All your welth will away,
>>> Thus I warn yow.
> Think how bair thow was borne, and bair ay will be,
> For oucht that sedis of thi self in ony sessoun;
> Thy cude (*baptismal cloth*), they claithis,
>> nor thi cost, cummis nocht of the,
> Bot of the frute of the erd, and Godis fosoun (*bounty*).
> Quhen ilk thing has the awne, suthly we se,
> Thy nakit cors bot of clay, a foule carioun,
> Hatit and hawless (*destitute*): quhar of art thow hie?
> We cum pure, we gang pure, baith king and commoun.
> Bot thow reule the richtwis (*justly*), thi roume sall orere!
>> (*kingdom will decline*)

These are fairly conventional sentiments, but again they derive greater force from their context. Holland has devoted much of his poem to praise of the Douglas family, recalling the role of James Douglas in the winning of Scottish independence, and there is an implied contrast between the natural nobility which he exemplifies and the acquired, undeserved estate of the aspiring Howlat. The *sententia* that we are all equally powerless in the sight of God no doubt applies to the Douglases as well as to the King; but the last line of the Howlat's lament seems to be directed at a royal listener. The fall of the Howlat may, as has recently been suggested, refer to the fall of the Livingston family which quickly followed the end of James II's minority, but it is equally the case that the poem is an apologia for the Douglas interest and may in that sense be an attempt to forestall an attack by the King on the Livingstons' erstwhile allies. If so, it was unsuccessful: in June 1452, the Earl of Moray and his wife were among the members of the Douglas family who were deprived of their titles and charged with treason.

In these two works, we can in different ways see how current political issues might influence the relationship of patronage between a king or magnate and a poet in his household. In a more general way, the authors of such poems as *Lancelot of the Laik*, *The Thre Prestis of Peblis* and *The Talis of The Fyve Bestes*, all of which probably belong to the second half of the fifteenth century, and Robert Henryson in his *Morall Fabillis*, can be seen to have been offering political advice to the Scottish king. The preoccupation of Middle Scots poets with the need for effective government is not confined to any one reign, and was doubtless due in large measure to the succession of minorities which complicated Scottish politics and which meant that for a total of

*J*ames I of Scotland who reigned 1406–37, with his Queen,
Joan Beaufort.

almost forty years in the fifteenth century – and for more than half the sixteenth century – power was in the hands of governors rather than the monarch himself. The remedies which the poets of loyal advice advocated were for the most part the traditional objectives of medieval political theory: the personal integrity of the ruler, reliance on prudent advisers, the even-handed administration of justice; but the insistence with which the themes are repeated suggests that the poets in and around the court were articulating a concern which had its basis in the realities of political life. Later medieval Scotland was probably no more disorderly or unjust than any other society of its day, but the problems of ineffective government certainly were a constant preoccupation.

It is striking that the reign in which these problems have been supposed to have been at their most acute was that of James III (1460–88), whose reputation as an unusually wilful and arbitrary king was established as early as the reign of his grandson and who certainly did provoke his magnates into an uprising which ended with his death at or after the battle of Sauchieburn. A painstaking study of his character and policies by Norman Macdougall has recently tended to confirm many of these harsh judgments; yet it is true that the court over which James III presided was probably the most cultured that Scotland had seen, and that his servants included several of unusual distinction. To some extent, these two sides of his personality are integrated in the sixteenth-century tradition that it was James' attachment to artists which provoked the magnates into a coup in 1482, but the culturally significant figures in the royal household were not the supposed architect Cochrane or the elusive musician William Roger but the Secretary Archibald Whitelaw and William Scheves, Archbishop of St Andrews.

The foundations of the court circle of James III were actually laid very early in his minority, when government was in the hands of the Dowager Queen, Mary of Gueldres. Whitelaw, who was to remain Secretary for over thirty years, was appointed to the office in the summer of 1462, having briefly served as Clerk Register. Also acquiring a position of power at this period was David Guthrie of Kincaldrum, Whitelaw's former pupil at the University of Cologne, while the Secretary's successor as Clerk Register, Fergus Makdowell, had probably been an acquaintance at St Andrews. Richard Guthrie, another Cologne graduate, was confessor to the young King at about the same time.

This group undoubtedly shared a common intellectual inheritance, deriving from the influential Albertist teacher, John Athilmer, who taught at St Andrews (1426–30), Cologne (1430–37), St Andrews (1438–41), Cologne again (1442–47), and finally at St Andrews again, from 1448 until his death in 1474. From 1450, he was Provost of St Salvator's College within the University of St Andrews. Although he was occasionally one of the ecclesiastical representatives in Parliament, Athilmer's contribution to Scottish government was principally through his students, the most distinguished of whom was probably Whitelaw, himself a master at Cologne for several years in the 1440s.

Serving for at least part of James' minority as tutor to the young King, Whitelaw must have had a considerable influence upon his master's cultural interests. Whitelaw himself was a collector of both manuscripts and printed books, with a particular interest in Roman antiquities; there is some evidence that manuscripts written for him were given at least a superficial gloss of humanist style. But he also had a practical administrator's concern for the law, and the one surviving canon law manuscript which he owned is copiously annotated in his hand, especially the section dealing with feudal tenure.

Whitelaw's career makes a striking contrast with that of William Scheves, a somewhat younger graduate of St Andrews who was not among those who achieved their position during James' minority. Scheves did not enter the royal household until 1470, just after the King had taken over the government with a determination which rivalled that of his father twenty years earlier. He began as the King's physician, but within eight years he was Archbishop of St Andrews, and although he never held any of the major offices of state, he was arguably the most powerful individual after the King himself. He, too, was a collector of books, but his greatest interests, medical works and the Scottish chronicles, again contrast with Whitelaw's classicism. Sixteenth-century historians ascribed Scheves' influence over the King to occult practices, but the truth is probably that he was a clever politician of considerable intellectual gifts.

As Whitelaw may have helped to form James III's tastes and Scheves may have influenced them in the 1470s, the last years of the reign saw the rise to prominence of another intellectual force, the Paris theologian John Ireland, who had become one of the most important masters in the Collège de Navarre despite having fallen foul of the University authorities at St Andrews in 1459. Scheves' evident hatred of Ireland – James III had to write to the Pope on the latter's behalf, asking that he be taken out of Scheves' ecclesiastical jurisdiction – may have dated from that academic dispute when he was a teacher at St Andrews and Ireland a student; but the fact is that Ireland reappeared in Scotland in 1479–80, where he was immediately taken up by the King and set to writing theological treatises, and after the death of Louis XI of France in 1483 he became a permanent member of the Scottish royal household, serving as royal confessor and acting as one of the Lords of Council.

Despite the many differences between them, Whitelaw, Scheves and Ireland all testify to the vital intellectual life of the royal court under James III. The King certainly paid for the production of at least one literary manuscript, a copy of *Mandeville's Travels* written by John

*The device of Andrew Myllar, who, with Walter Chapman, was permitted by James IV to establish Scotland's first printing press in 1507.*

Blair in 1467, and it has credibly been suggested that the royal copy of the *Aeneid*, now Edinburgh University Library MS. 195, was written for him. Another commission from the end of the reign has a poignant ring: the copy of Magninus' *Regimen sanitatis*, which was written by the successful commercial scribe Magnus Makculloch at Leith and finished on Maundy Thursday 1487, was produced for John Ramsay, Lord Bothwell, then at the height of his newly acquired power as a protégé of the King, who was within eighteen months to become the scapegoat for the maladministration of James III and on that account to lose his lordship.

It is easy to believe that within such a court circle, whatever tensions may have existed between its members, the poems of Robert Henryson received an appreciative response. There is no evidence to associate Henryson, who very probably taught at the University of Glasgow (which was itself to a large extent an offshoot of the St Andrews-Cologne Albertist axis) in 1462 and was certainly active in Dunfermline in 1478, with the royal court; but his *Morall Fabillis* are addressed in part to kings and lords, and Henryson claims that his adaptations from 'Esope' were made 'be requeist and precept of ane lord'. This anonymous patron may be no more than a conventional device, yet the principles of good government which are enunciated in *The Lyoun and the Mous* and reinforced in other fables are essentially those of the advice tradition, while the witty, learned manner of the *Fabillis* and the familiarity with Chaucerian poetry, which enhances an understanding of *The Testament of Cresseid*, surely imply the sort of sophisticated audience which the court provided. We must beware of too easy an assumption that Henryson wrote expressly for James III and his circle, but the milieu of Whitelaw, Scheves and the learned Dr Ireland was one which would have appreciated the blend of urbane humour and rather stern morality which characterise his poems.

If the relationship between Henryson and the royal court is somewhat equivocal, there is no doubt concerning the position of William Dunbar under James IV. In what has been described as 'the aureate age', the courtier-poet enjoyed a public prominence (if not, in Dunbar's case at least, prosperity) much more obvious than would seem to have been available to Henryson and his anonymous contemporaries. Nor was Dunbar the only beneficiary of this overt royal patronage: Gavin Douglas, although his translation of the *Aeneid* was commissioned not by the King but, as we have seen, by Lord Sinclair, dedicated his *Palice of Honour* to James IV and may have received the provostship of the church of St Giles in Edinburgh in recompense. John Ireland was another to seek the King's support, marking the beginning of the reign by offering James a theological and political primer in Scots, which was entitled *The Meroure of Wysdome*.

It is Dunbar, however, who dominates his generation as Henryson had dominated his, and again the contrast is instructive. Whereas Henryson is generally measured in his tone, stylistically restrained and consistently didactic, Dunbar's technical virtuosity has become a critical commonplace. His attention to rhetorical display and his command of a wide variety of styles and modes sometimes overshadow the content of his verse, and he has often been regarded as a court entertainer with relatively little to say.

It is true that Dunbar is a master of comic verse, and that we gain from his poems an insight into the familiar life of the court with a concreteness which is unique in Scots. His playful, mocking references to his contemporaries illuminate the shadowy world of the Treasurer's Accounts, giving reality to an intimate circle of which we would otherwise know little. But even here there is a darker side; the two poems which Dunbar wrote against the alchemist John Damian, who attempted to fly from the walls of Stirling Castle with a pair of feathered wings in 1507, is animated by a fairly venomous animosity, which may in part reflect the traditional mistrust of scientific experiment but which also reveals the poet's hatred of a rival for the patronage of the King.

The lightness of Dunbar's touch can often be deceptive, and his reliance on his audience's familiarity with the nuances of the conventional images he deploys can cause the modern reader to miss the subtlety of the argument. Thus the poem which he wrote for the marriage of James IV and Margaret Tudor in 1503, *The Thrissill and the Rois*, is much more than a formal celebration of a state occasion, although its final paean of praise for the Rois (the allegorical representation of the English princess) is clearly intended to mark the event with a full-scale rhetorical climax.

In the central narrative section of the poem, in which Nature invests the Lyoun, the Egle and the Thrissill with the office of kingship, Dunbar joins the ranks of the poets of political advice, advocating the equitable administration of justice and urging James to use his royal power to protect the weak in society against the depredations of the mighty. This traditional counsel is combined with the more personal advice we noticed at the outset: the Thrissill is instructed by Nature to set aside the vile nettles and to remain faithful to the 'fresche Rois'. Such an emphasis on the personal morality of the sovereign was timely and no doubt justified, but it was also traditional; medieval political themes emphasised the close relationship between the private integrity of the monarch and the public well-being of the realm.

Dunbar frames his vision of the new political dispensation of Dame Nature within a familiar convention of high style poetry: he has been upbraided by May, he tells us, for having failed to write the celebratory Spring poem which he had promised. His response is that the weather is not as literary tradition declares it should be:

> Thy air it is nocht holsum nor benyn
> Lord Eolus dois in thy sessone ring;
> So busteous ar the blastis of his horne
> Amang thy bewis to walk I haif forborne.

May's answer to this complaint is to lead him into the dream-garden in which he witnesses Nature's parliament, and the point is the new

*The Nova Felix Arabia Arch, erected for the entry of James VI into London. The nine muses and the seven liberal arts represented flatter the new monarch's intellectual achievements.*

harmony in the natural world which is to be brought about by the arrival of the Rois. This really is a new beginning, and the climatic discussion of the opening stanzas takes on a political significance as we understand the force of the orders which Nature gives. Here is the court poet at his best, taking the conceits of fashionable verse and giving them fresh meaning in a poem which both compliments the patron and offers a serious comment upon the implications of contemporary events.

The importance of the court as a centre of literary activity did not end with the disaster at Flodden, although Dunbar is never heard of again and the political factionalism of the minority which followed drove Gavin Douglas into exile in England. The household of the infant James V included Sir David Lindsay, whose poems of entertainment and advice continued the tradition of the courtier-poet. In his adulthood, James V, too, was a notable patron, commissioning from John Bellenden translations of Livy and of the Scottish historian Hector Boece, which rank among the more notable achievements of Scots prose.

Lindsay, despite his strong commitment to the Reforming cause, remained an influential figure during the minority and absence in France of Queen Mary, right up to his death in 1555. Also prominent at court in this period was Alexander Scott, whose *New Yeir Gift* (1562) provides a fascinating record of a moderate's reaction to the upheavals of the Reformation, while Sir Richard Maitland, though less accomplished as a poet, wrote prolifically on matters of state throughout the middle part of the century.

It was in the reign of James VI, however, that the Scottish court reached its fullest development as a literary centre. Influenced by his poetic mentor, Alexander Montgomerie, James VI set out to establish a new school of Scots verse and his 'Castalian Band' flourished during the 1580s. Translations were made from Ariosto and Machiavelli, while the sonnet was adopted as the most versatile form for lyric verse. Both as a poet and as a patron, James VI was the most ambitious of the Stewart kings, but the dependence of the literary culture upon the court was to prove disastrous when he inherited the English crown in 1603. Thereafter, there was no focus for court culture in Scotland, and the virtual disappearance of serious poetry in Scots after 1603 was a direct result, to a very considerable degree, of the movement of the court to London.

The Scottish kings had helped to provide a setting for the development of a distinctive national literature in Scots from the end of the fourteenth century, one which had celebrated the achievements of the Scottish nation and commented upon its difficulties. It would, of course, be wrong to suggest that everything of importance written in Scotland between 1375 and 1603 was even indirectly political; but the court with its particular preoccupations was a source of patronage and an appreciative audience throughout the Middle Scots period.

The last word should perhaps go to the quintessential court poet, Dunbar, who for all his plaintive petitioning knew that it was upon the King that he must rely:

> The formest hoip yit that I have
> In all this warld, sa God me save,
> Is in your Grace, bayth crop and grayne,
>     Quhilk is ane lessing of my pane.

# CHAPTER IV

# 'Scotching the Brut':
# The Early History of Britain

ROGER A. MASON

I n the Picture Gallery of the Palace of Holyroodhouse in Edinburgh, there hang the portraits of 111 Scottish kings. Commissioned by Charles II in 1684 and painted by a Dutch artist, Jacob de Wet, this curious collection encompasses almost exactly two millennia of Scotland's royal history. Beginning with Fergus I, whose foundation of the Scottish kingdom was alleged to have occurred in 330 BC, the portraits chronicle in unbroken succession each subsequent generation of the Scottish royal line down to Charles II himself and his brother, the future James VII and II.

Undistinguished though the paintings are, it would be wrong to dismiss them simply as evidence of the Stewart dynasty's overweening pride in a long and largely fabricated pedigree. They also provide an outstanding visual record of an historical mythology which for several centuries played a critical role in the development of Scottish national consciousness. Whatever Charles II's interest in them may have been, the long and illustrious line of kings symbolised for the generality of Scottish subjects not so much the antiquity of Stewart kingship as the autonomy of the Scottish kingdom. In fact, the ancient race of kings – and particularly its forty mythical representatives – served a crucial ideological function throughout the later Middle Ages and well into the early modern period. For as symbols of Scotland's original and continuing independence, they supplied a vital counterweight to an English historiographical tradition which, stemming from the twelfth-century Welsh cleric Geoffrey of Monmouth, insisted that Scotland was and always had been a dependency of the crown of England.

Among the many intriguing puzzles surrounding Geoffrey of Monmouth's *History of the Kings of Britain* is why a compilation of Welsh legend should have appealed so strongly to the Anglo-Norman peoples of post-Conquest England. But appeal it certainly did and for several centuries – and with no apparent sense of irony – the English appropriated to themselves the heroic exploits of a British race whose Welsh descendants they were rather less inclined to honour. In this way, Arthur and Merlin, Lear and Cymbeline became part-and-parcel of English tradition, while English chroniclers long believed that Britain was first ruled by Brutus, great-grandson of the Trojan Aeneas, who gave his

*The* Historia Regum Britannia, *Geoffrey of Monmouth's twelfth-century history.*

name both to the island and to its original inhabitants. In short, however paradoxically, the British History – or Brut tradition – came to form the basis of a long-lived and remarkably influential English national epos.

There is no doubt, for example, that it informs almost all the many versions of English history which poured from the press in the century following Caxton's pioneering publication of the *Chronicle of England* (1480) and the *Polychronicon* (1482) – both of them saturated in exotic Galfridian lore. There were, of course, critics of the tradition, most notably the humanist scholar Polydore Vergil whose *Anglica Historia* first appeared in 1534. But Polydore was after all a mere Italian and his sceptical approach to early British history was brushed contemptuously aside in the stridently patriotic chronicles of such later Tudor historians as Hall, Grafton and Holinshed. Moreover, the hapless Polydore was clearly tinged with Romish prejudice and thus highly suspect as a source for an English history rapidly assuming garishly Protestant hues. By the end of the sixteenth century, the works of Bale, Parker and Foxe had adapted the British History to an apocalyptic timescale and, deftly combining patriotism with Protestantism, had given rise to the extraordinarily powerful conviction that England was an Elect Nation – that God, as Bishop Aylmer proclaimed, was Himself English – and that the imperial English monarchy had a leading role in that cosmic drama whose imminent *dénouement* would see the final destruction of the papal Antichrist.

That the Scots were less than happy with this canonical version of English history is hardly surprising. For although only implicit in Geoffrey of Monmouth's original work, his many disciples elaborated the British History in such a way as to make quite explicit their belief that the Scottish kingdom was subject to the crown of England. This claim to feudal superiority rested on three main arguments. Firstly, it was said to be inherent in the division of the British kingdom which occurred on the death of its founding father, Brutus the Trojan. For, conveniently enough, Brutus had had three sons, the eldest of whom, Locrinus, inherited England, while the second, Kamber, inherited Wales, and the third, Albanactus, inherited Scotland. Thus England's seniority among the British monarchies was made clear from the very outset.

In case this original proof of English precedence failed to impress, however, the Brut chroniclers could readily marshal a second and apparently still more conclusive argument. For was it not universally acknowledged that that glorious prince King Arthur had held sway over a vast sixth-century empire which encompassed not only the British Isles – Scotland being a tributary kingdom – but also Scandinavia and Gaul? Surely an unassailable precedent which the Scots were bound to concede. But just to confirm their dependency, a third argument was advanced which was to figure particularly prominently in the debates sparked off by the union of the crowns in 1603 and even to feature in the pamphlet wars which raged at the time of the parliamentary union of 1707. That is, that throughout the Middle Ages Scottish kings had habitually done homage to their English counterparts and thereby quite openly acknowledged that they and their subjects owed allegiance ultimately to the crown of England.

Much as they may have wanted to, the Scots could not afford simply to dismiss these arguments as delusions of the English imperial mind. After all, thus interpreted, the British History was of much more than academic significance: it was an ideological weapon which English kings could – and did – draw upon to underwrite armed aggression against the Scots. In the 1290s, for example, Edward I made good use of the Brut tradition when charged by Pope Boniface VIII to justify his attempted subjugation of the northern realm. Similarly, in the 1540s, on the eve of one of his many Scottish campaigns, Henry VIII issued a *Declaration* (1542) which deployed the whole panoply of the British History (including Brutus and his progeny) in order to demonstrate his right to the sovereignty of Scotland. Such examples could be multiplied, but it will be clear enough already that the Scots had good grounds for resenting the imperialist construction which the British History could be made to carry and good grounds too for concocting a version of their own past which would demonstrate conclusively that the imperial ambitions of their English neighbours had no historical justification whatsoever.

They wasted little time in doing so. A counter-mythology was clearly taking shape as early as the thirteenth century and was drawn upon both in the Scots' reply to Edward I's submission to the papal curia and some years later in the opening paragraph of that masterly piece of diplomatic rhetoric, the *Declaration of Arbroath* (1320). But it was not in fact fully formulated until later in the fourteenth century when, between 1384 and 1387, John of Fordun, a chantry priest in the cathedral church of Aberdeen, compiled the first version of what was to become known as the *Scotichronicon*. Needless to say, Fordun was acutely conscious of the invidious implications of the British History and throughout his work was at pains to confound what he called 'the foolish babbling of the British people'. For a start he denied categorically that Brutus had ruled over and given his name to the whole of the British Isles. Rather, he insisted in no uncertain terms that the correct name for the whole island was in fact Albion, while Britain referred only to that part of it – now also known as England – where Brutus had actually ruled. With Brutus thus safely confined to the southern parts of Albion, his son Albanactus was rendered harmless and Fordun could move on to the other arguments which sustained the English imperial case. He gave them short shrift: Arthur's allegedly pan-European empire was met with a deafeningly eloquent silence, while any examples of Scottish kings doing homage to their English counterparts were dismissed as involving only the lands they held in England and not their kingdom as a whole.

Having answered the case for English superiority in this way, Fordun then went on to develop an interpretation of the Scottish past which he hoped would free it once and for all from the incubus of the Brut tradition. Thus, according to Fordun's account, the progenitors of the Scottish race were a Greek prince named Gathelus (the Greeks did after all defeat the Trojans!) and the eponymous Scota, daughter of Pharaoh, whom Gathelus married shortly before Moses delivered the children of Israel out of Egypt. In the wake of the Pharaoh's destruction in the Red Sea, Gathelus and Scota were forced to flee from Egypt and, after roaming the Mediterranean for a time, they eventually settled in Spain. From Spain, their descendants colonised first Ireland and then Dalriada

(Argyll) in the hitherto uninhabited – that is, non-British – west of Scotland in the fifth century BC. From being a colony, Dalriada was eventually made into an independent kingdom – replete with the hallowed Stone of Destiny – under Fergus I, son of Ferchard, in 330 BC. This kingdom, Fordun maintained, endured for seven centuries under forty anonymous kings until the Romans, in league with the Picts, overthrew it in AD 360. But the breach was only temporary and in AD 403 Fergus II, son of Erc, refounded the kingdom which in the eighth century was extended to encompass that of the Picts and over which, despite the best endeavours of their English neighbours, Fergus' descendants had reigned as independent monarchs down to Fordun's own day.

Clearly, this picturesque narrative, partly derived from Irish legend, was a quite deliberate attempt to scotch the imperialist history emanating from the English court. The Scottish kingdom was, it implied, among the oldest in Europe and its independence – unlike that of England – was

*'Diana's Response to Brut', the frontispiece to the Temple Classic edition of Monmouth's history, published in 1903.*

unsullied by either conquest or feudal submission. In effect, Fordun had elaborated a Scottish national epos which, paralleling that of Geoffrey of Monmouth, could be used to counter the latter's Anglo-centric interpretation of early British history. Not unexpectedly, therefore, the Scots found Fordun's chronicle highly congenial and north of the border the *Scotichronicon* held its own throughout the fifteenth and well into the sixteenth century. Fordun's work was not, however, the last word on the subject. For in 1527, Hector Boece, the distinguished first principal of the University of Aberdeen, published his *Scotorum Historiae*, a quite remarkable work in which the Scottish national epos assumed its final and most extravagant form.

The chronology of the *Scotorum Historiae* is based directly on Fordun, and Boece followed his predecessor in painstakingly refuting the British History whenever it impugned either the autonomy or the antiquity of the Scottish kingdom. In this respect, in fact, Boece added little that was new. Where he came into his own was in his lengthy account of those obscure seven centuries between the first foundation of the kingdom by Fergus I in 330 BC and its refoundation by Fergus II in AD 403. These centuries had been left virtually blank by Fordun – for the very good reason that the Irish Scots did not in fact colonise Dalriada before the fifth century AD. Boece, however, claiming like Geoffrey of Monmouth to have had access to sources which were never to be seen again, proceeded not only to name all forty of the hitherto anonymous kings of Dalriada, but also to describe with a wealth of circumstantial detail both their warlike deeds and the workings of the polity over which they ruled. It was from this wholly fictitious part of Boece's narrative that, later in the sixteenth century, George Buchanan drew the examples of resistance and tyrannicide which proved so useful as precedents for the deposition of Mary Stewart in 1567. It is unlikely, however, that Boece intended them as illustrations of any such constitutional principle. To him, they served rather the more modest and essentially moral-cum-patriotic purpose of exemplifying the fate of vicious kings whose corrupt and cowardly behaviour posed a threat to the integrity of the realm.

Far from being a radical political tract, therefore, Boece's chronicle is in fact an intensely conservative celebration of the martial virtues which he believed had ensured the freedom of the Scottish realm since its very foundation. It is this theme which lends the *Scotorum Historiae* its considerable narrative power. For, according to Boece, when all Europe succumbed to the might of the Roman legions and groaned under the yoke of imperial tutelage, Scotland alone succeeded in preserving her freedom and, in a long and noble struggle, never once submitted to slavery and subjection. While the kings of the Britons became puppets of the Roman emperors and thereafter fell in rapid succession to the Saxons, the Danes and finally the Normans, the Scots – led by their illustrious race of kings – resisted the Romans, exterminated the Picts, briefly subjugated the Britons, repulsed the Danes and for centuries refused to recognise the baseless claims to superiority made by a succession of arrogant English monarchs. By our standards, of course, it is all thoroughly bad history. But then so too were the Brut chronicles to which Boece provided a fitting, if somewhat belated, riposte.

At least within Scotland, Boece proved immensely popular and the *Scotorum Historiae* remained the standard work in the field until the publication in 1582 of Buchanan's *Rerum Scoticarum Historia*. Yet even within Scotland, the tradition Boece espoused was not without its critics. A few years before Boece's work appeared, the great scholastic theologian John Mair had entered the historical debate in a manner which was hardly calculated to please his fellow countrymen. For if in his *Historia Majoris Britanniae* (1521) he lambasted Caxton for speaking of the Scots 'in language that held as many lies as it did words', he nevertheless went on to ditch Gathelus and Scota – and much else besides – quite as summarily as he ditched Brutus and his wretched progeny. As far as Mair was concerned, the legendary histories of both countries were ridiculous and, although he would have no truck with the English claim to superiority over Scotland, neither did he sympathise with the Scots' xenophobic attitude to England. In fact, as the title of his book suggests, Mair was an unashamed advocate of union and looked forward to the creation of a British monarchy, not through war and conquest, but through a series of dynastic marriages which would in time unite the hitherto sovereign crowns of Scotland and England in the person of a single ruler.

Mair's wish was, of course, eventually to be fulfilled when in 1603 James VI of Scotland fell heir also to the throne of England. But in the early sixteenth century such an outcome looked less than likely. Indeed, in the 1530s, Henry VIII's desperate search for a Tudor heir to his English kingdom set in motion a train of events with monumental and potentially highly divisive consequences for the British monarchies. For the English break with Rome and the spread of Protestantism through her political establishment placed Scotland in a delicate but strategically crucial position on the European stage. Her diplomatic ties and confessional allegiance suddenly, if quite fortuitously, assumed unprecedented significance and much came to depend on whether she too would break with Rome and, severing the ancient alliance with Catholic France, realign herself with Protestant England. In this new context and particularly under Protestant influence, the idea of union was broadcast with renewed intensity and with far-reaching implications. Yet it was not the union of equal partners envisaged by Mair, it was union based rather on the Scots' 'domestication' within a revamped and explicitly

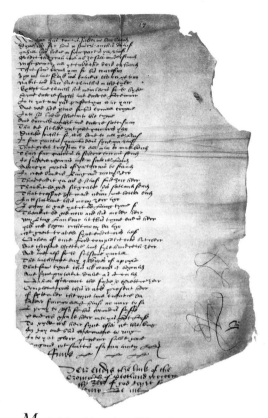

*M*etrical *Scottish version of Hector Boece's* Scotorum
Historiae *(Buik of the Croniclis of Scotland) produced in the 1530s.*

Protestantised British History – that is, it was union based on the Scots' acceptance of their historic position as a subject people owing allegiance to an English – or British – crown which was both Protestant as well as imperial.

The critical decade in the formation of this British unionist ideology was undoubtedly the 1540s. To English eyes, the death of James V in 1542 leaving as his heir the week-old Mary Queen of Scots provided a golden opportunity to gain control of Scottish affairs through the betrothal of Mary to Henry VIII's son and heir, Prince Edward. The Scots were understandably suspicious and, although they initially agreed to the match, they later reneged, thus initiating the bloody conflict known as the 'Rough Wooing'. To Henry himself, these Scottish wars were little more than a dynastic power-play. To many of his subjects, however, they assumed the character of a Protestant crusade and were prosecuted with a self-righteous ferocity born of the conviction that the Scots were obstructing a providentially arranged marriage which was part of a divine plan to overthrow the papal powers of darkness. This apocalyptic vision reached the peak of its intensity with the death of Henry VIII in 1547 and the accession of the 'godly' Edward VI under the protection of the Duke of Somerset. The same year saw Somerset's crushing defeat of the Scots at the battle of Pinkie and his subsequent occupation of the Lowlands. This military campaign was accompanied by a barrage of propaganda of which the most interesting example for our purposes was written by James Henryson, a substantial Edinburgh merchant who in 1547 published *An Exhortation to the Scots to conform themselves to the honourable, expedient & godly union between the realms of England & Scotland.*

Henryson's primary aim in his pamphlet was to persuade the Scots that the proposed marriage would not lead simply to a fortuitous dynastic union but would mark above all the final re-creation of a British monarchy 'as it was first and yet still ought to be'. Not unexpectedly, this claim was based four-square on the British History and Henryson not only endorsed the historicity of the Brutus legend, but went on to rehearse all twenty-two examples of the Scots doing homage to English superiors as set down in Henry VIII's *Declaration* of 1542. More significantly, however, Henryson also went out of his way to emphasise – *pace* Fordun and Boece – that the whole of the British Isles had been conquered by the Romans and to focus attention firmly on the heroic figure of Constantine the Great, the first Christian emperor, but also, and crucially, a king of the Britons.

The belief that Constantine was of British birth and descent was part-and-parcel of the Brut tradition and Henryson was merely following Geoffrey of Monmouth in arguing that the emperor was the son of the Roman general Constancius who, through his marriage to Helen, daughter and heir of Coel, king of the Britons, had gained possession of the British throne. Constantine's claim to the kingship of Britain was therefore based on birth as well as on conquest.

More importantly, however, if in Constantine were united both British kingship and Roman emperorship, then arguably his successors in Britain fell heir not just to his kingdom but also to his imperial status. In other words, Constantine provided an invaluable precedent for the complete jurisdictional self-sufficiency – the imperial status – which the English crown claimed when Henry VIII repudiated Rome and assumed the headship of the church in England. Yet Henryson did not have recourse to the Brut simply to underwrite the Henrician royal supremacy. He did so with the further aim of fixing Scotland securely within the orbit of the same imperial crown. Thus the centrality of Constantine to his vision of the past is founded on the conviction, persistently reiterated, that 'he had all Britain in possession'. Accordingly, the empire of Constantine's successors, of Henry VIII and Edward VI, was not merely English, it was British. Moreover, given the proposed marriage of Edward to Mary, Scotsmen too could participate in the imperial and Protestant future which the breach with Rome inaugurated.

Needless to say, such a unionist ideology was far removed from that promulgated by John Mair. To effect union and at the same time to further the Protestant faith, the Scots were now being asked to jettison their time-honoured belief in Scotland's original and continuing autonomy and to accept rather her dependent status within a redefined British imperial framework. It proved too much for the majority of Scots to swallow and in 1548 Mary Stewart was conveyed to France and to an eventual French marriage. Yet this was by no means the end of the story. In the 1560s, for example, many reforming Scots – including John Knox – advocated dynastic union with England in terms closely akin to those elaborated by Henryson, while later in the century James VI was increasingly cast in the role of the long-awaited British Constantine. But the British History never attained widespread acceptance in Scotland, even among Protestant Anglophiles. George Buchanan, for example, despite being a supporter of a Protestant and Anglophile Scottish government and despite being the tutor of a future British king, has to be numbered among the British History's most searching critics.

At least in part, Buchanan's *Rerum Scoticarum Historia* (1582) was written to lend historical legitimacy to the radical political ideology which he had developed to justify Mary Stewart's deposition in 1567. Based squarely on Boece's chronicle, the reigns of many of the mythi-

*Scota, daughter of Pharaoh, arriving in Scotland in the fifth century BC, from Fordun's* Scotichronicon.

cal kings described there were construed by Buchanan as illustrating
the constitutionality of resistance and even of regicide. Small wonder,
then, that Buchanan took such exception to Humphrey Lhuyd, a Welsh
antiquary who in 1572 published a work in which he denounced Boece
as 'a malicious falsifier without all shame or honesty' and proceeded
quite justifiably to deny the very existence of a Scottish realm – far
less a line of forty kings – before the fifth century AD. Yet there is
more to Buchanan's vitriolic attack on Lhuyd than this suggests. After
all, Buchanan's political theory was founded in natural law rather than
prescriptive right and so Boece's kings were in that respect merely a
convenience, not a necessity. They were a necessity, however, if the
antiquity and autonomy of the Scottish realm were not finally to fall
victim to the blandishments of a Welshman who, for all his scepticism
about the Scottish past, remained nevertheless a staunch upholder of
Geoffrey of Monmouth and that same Brut tradition which Boece had
sought to counter. It was not, therefore, simply Buchanan's radical
political principles which were at stake, there was also the question
of his patriotic pride.

Of course, by this time it was impossible for an urbane humanist of
Buchanan's stature to peddle a legend like that of Gathelus and Scota
and he very sensibly laid it quickly and quietly to rest. His destruction
of Brutus and his sons, however, was both a much noisier and a much
lengthier affair. It was, moreover, one that elicited his most valuable
contribution to antiquarian studies, for in order to expose what he called
the 'enormous falsehoods' of Geoffrey of Monmouth and Humphrey
Lhuyd, Buchanan brought to bear his considerable philological expertise
in an argument which demonstrated that both Scots and Britons had
somewhat more humble origins among the tribes of ancient Gaul. In
the course of this expert analysis, the Brut legend with all its imperial
pretensions was effectively exploded. Thereafter, however, Buchanan's
critical sense deserted him. He simply would not accept Lhuyd's argument that the first seven centuries of Scottish history as retold by Boece
were pure fabrication. To be sure, Boece was at times absurdly fanciful,
but his chronology was perfectly correct: the Scottish kingdom was
founded by Fergus, son of Ferchard, in 330 BC and – despite the
imperialist assumptions of Arthurian enthusiasts and misguided English
medievalists – had had a continuous and independent existence ever since
that date. Clearly, Buchanan was as keen to vindicate the honour of
his native realm as any of his predecessors. His *Historia* is not simply
the work of a radical political ideologue, but also that of a convinced
Scottish patriot.

Nevertheless, despite his vigorous endorsement of the Scottish
national epos, Buchanan was by no means an unrepentant Anglophobe.
On the contrary, he was prepared to look favourably on the idea of

union with England. Yet he clearly would not have gone along with Henryson in denying Scotland's historic sovereign status. Like Mair, in fact, Buchanan expected union to be one of equal partners involving an explicit recognition of Scotland's autonomy. In this respect, his views were shared by Sir Thomas Craig, the great Scottish lawyer and philosopher of union who, even as union was finally realised in 1603, felt obliged to write a sizeable tome defending Scotland from what he called the 'fooleries and scurrilities' contained in Raphael Holinshed's chronicles of 1577. With vast erudition, the British History was once more taken to task and Brutus, Arthur and all the medieval precedents for homage were once more exposed as delusions of the English imperial mind. Predictably enough, however, Craig could not bring himself to dump Boece's lengthy line of ancient Scottish kings. Certainly, stout royalist that he was, their reigns had to be purged of Buchanan's radicalism. However, the line itself was sacrosanct – an ongoing symbol of Scotland's historic freedom.

Despite his best endeavours, however, Craig remained uneasily aware that the English were unlikely to be impressed by James VI's distinguished pedigree – and unlikely either to see union as a means of sinking ancient enmities in the creation of a truly British realm on the lines first envisaged by Mair. For that, among other things, would have required the writing of a truly British history. But why bother? Secure in the knowledge of their own election, their past already so compellingly chronicled in Foxe's *Book of Martyrs*, the English had no desire to rewrite their history to accommodate the Scots. Despite the revolution in antiquarian studies inaugurated by Camden's *Britannia* (1586), most Englishmen and indeed many Scots found it both easier and more satisfying to hail the first British king as Constantine *redivivus* than as the lineal descendant of Fergus MacFerchard. Boece's kings, therefore, and the national epos associated with them, were hard-pressed to survive the seventeenth century.

Although championed in the 1680s by the redoubtable royalist lawyer, Sir George Mackenzie, Jacob de Wet's work on Holyroodhouse failed to reinvigorate a now untenable mythology. Treated with scant respect in the controversial literature generated by the parliamentary union of 1707, the early kings were finally laid to rest in 1729 when Father Thomas Innes published his *Critical Essay on the Ancient Inhabitants of the Northern Parts of Britain*. Although an exemplary record scholar, however, Innes was also a fervent Jacobite. As a result, unwilling to deny the Stewarts some semblance of an immemorial pedigree, he substituted for the ancient line of Scottish kings, the still older and lengthier line of the Pictish royal house. Perhaps fortunately, this resplendent genealogy had little future among the 'enlightened' Scottish historians who flourished in the wake of the '45.

# CHAPTER V

# The Nobility of Jacobean Scotland 1567–1625

KEITH M. BROWN

In July 1567 a powerful faction of the Scottish nobility forced Mary Queen of Scots to abdicate, and in her place crowned her infant son, James VI. This revolution marked the nadir in the decline of the Stewart monarchy, a decline which began in 1542, and underlined the growth in power of a nobility thought to have been tamed by the crown in the fifteenth century. While James II had smashed the great Douglas family in the 1450s in an impressive and frightening display of arbitrary royal authority, the nobility of the mid-sixteenth century had carried out a Protestant reformation in 1560 in defiance of the crown, and seven years later had replaced the monarch herself. Furthermore, when intellectuals like John Knox, George Buchanan and Andrew Melville could seize on history and scripture to justify, even to encourage such actions, men could be forgiven for wondering whether Scotland was 'mair nor a monarque' or 'les then electywe'.

Yet Scotland was neither Poland nor Venice, and neither the monarchy nor the Stewart dynasty was ever threatened. The noble dominated minorities which followed governed through crown offices, and regents like Moray and Morton acted like reigning kings, and expected to be regarded as such. When James came of age, the apparatus of monarchy was handed over intact, even if his revenues were somewhat depleted. Foreign observers, domestic commentators, and even the King himself might draw attention to the enormous power of the Scottish nobility, but one should never lose sight of the commitment of these nobles to a Stewart monarchy. As for James, he reminded his son in *Basilikon Doron* that 'virtue followeth oftest noble blood', and that it was they, the nobles, who 'must be your arms and executors of your laws'.

What conflict there was between crown and nobility in Jacobean Scotland never involved these fundamental attitudes. Unlike his mother, and his son Charles, James did not offend the nobility as a class, and was never collectively challenged by them. Nor, as some argue, did he attack his nobility as part of a grand absolutist strategy. When James died the means by which noble power was exercised might have altered, but the balance of power in the Scottish state still lay with them in their localities.

That is not to say that individual magnates were not brought low. In 1587–88 Lord Maxwell was exiled and later imprisoned, while between

1589 and 1595 the Earls of Huntly, Errol and Angus were defeated in a succession of royal campaigns in the north-east. All these men were militant Catholics who conspired with Spain to raise armed rebellion, yet they each believed that ultimately James would join them, or compromise with them, and none of them would face the King in the field. For his part, James refused Protestant clamouring for their heads, or even their lands, and, following their submission and nominal conformity, all were pardoned. He was less forgiving to his cousin, the Earl of Bothwell, a man with a largely justifiable reputation for violence, sorcery and audacious daring who both outraged and frightened the King. Bothwell was forfeited and, after four years of spectacular guerilla activities, he fled the kingdom for good. Yet in spite of an attempt by pro-Bothwell propagandists to persuade the nobility that 'The peril of one is the peril of all', his fellow peers did not share his mock solidarity, and except for kinsmen and short-term political allies, they united behind the King. There was no state building here, just old fashioned magnate politics with the spoils being divided accordingly; Bothwell's lands and jurisdictions being granted to the Duke of Lennox, Lord Hume, and the baronial chiefs of the Scott and Kerr kindreds.

Without the co-operation of the majority of his nobility, James could not have overcome Maxwell, Huntly and Bothwell. Nor could the crown have succeeded in reducing the level of violence in Scottish society. The pressure for such reform came first from the church, but while both King and nobility might have resented the ruthless vocabulary employed by ministers in condemning their laxity as magistrates, they agreed that something had to be done. The King's political theorising led to his own denunciation of private violence for more secular reasons – though he continued to approve of private justice – and the nobility was not immune to either of these criticisms, or to the on-going evolution of renaissance ideas about honour, nobility and civil society which were so at odds with the prevailing ideology of the bloodfeud.

The first attempts to restrain feuds, to outlaw duelling, and to restrict the carrying of firearms were in fact made by the minority governments. When James later built on that legislation, he did face some noble opposition, particularly over the anti-feuding act of 1598. However, the objections were not to royal efforts to control violence, but to the threat of royal interference in the localities and in private justice. When that threat failed to materialise, noble co-operation was secured, and James travelled south in 1603 with most of the great noble feuds laid to rest. Those few noblemen who did end up on the block – Lords Crichton and Maxwell (son of the above 8th lord), and the Earl of Orkney – did so because of the extreme nature of their crimes, and with the acquiescence of their peers. There is no doubt that the Scottish nobility earned their reputation for violence: the killing of Chancellor Glamis in 1579, the slaughter of the Earl of Eglinton in 1585, Huntly's brutal murder of the Earl of Moray in 1592, and the Earl of Cassillis' slaying of the Laird of Bargany in 1601 are only the more notorious among a long list of bloody deeds perpetrated by noblemen and their followers. Yet these same men were also officials, councillors and judges who were as concerned as any other ruling class to impose order and control violence, and it is a mistake to think that they had any self interest in protecting a level of violence which was clearly out of control. It is quite inconceivable to imagine that the crown alone, with only the most basic administrative and policing capabilities, or even in alliance with a largely illusive middle class, could have pacified Scotland in defiance of the nobility with their enormous influence in parliament and at court, and with their virtual monopoly of local government and policing.

While enforcing local law and order was a duty most noblemen took seriously, though not disinterestedly, and a privilege they guarded jealously, few were prepared to serve regularly in the royal administration at the centre. Court offices and household appointments were much sought after as they ensured a place close to the King for a magnate, or one of his clients. Thus in 1588 the captaincy of the guard was the bone of contention between the Lyon and Lindsay kindreds. However, the offices of state and positions in the administration of government aroused little enthusiasm. There were exceptions, as in the struggle for the chancellorship throughout the tenureship of John Maitland of Thirlstane when he had to fend off the claims of Bothwell, the Master of Glamis, and the Earl of Mar. Yet in 1585 the popular Presbyterian Earl of Angus was thought to have turned the office down in favour of local ambitions, and after Maitland's death, Mar refused to sacrifice local interests and take up an office the King clearly wanted him to have. Both men were typical in that the whole point of having office, or influence, was to increase, or protect, local interests; the office itself held few attractions, and could even be a burden. The Earl of Cassillis discovered this in 1599 when he was forced to give up the office of treasurer after only a few weeks because he found it too expensive to maintain.

Most men realised anyway that far more could be achieved through attendance at court, on a hunt, or in a late night drinking session with the King, than in long tedious hours at the council table. For that very reason the privy council waged a war on the chamber, and on the privy letters and commissions which were the results of such royal familiarity. In this the council scored some modest successes, but the motives of its members had as much to do with protecting their own control of the patronage flow as with any sympathy for absolutism. The desertion of Edinburgh by noblemen after 1603, and the growing influence of lawyers and bishops had little to do with policy, and everything to do with the whereabouts of the King and the court.

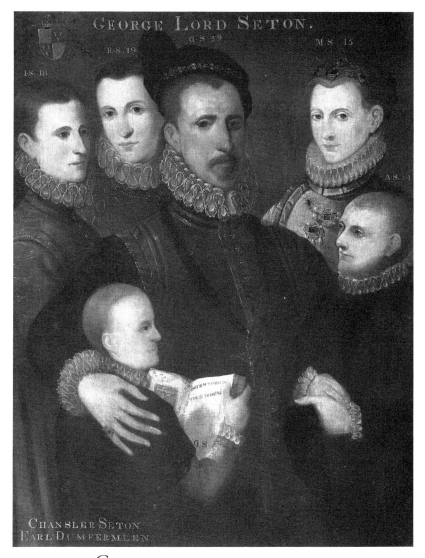

*George Seton, 5th Earl Seton, 1531–85, with his family.*
*This painting affords a rare insight into the domestic life of*
*the nobility.*

This is not to argue that noblemen did not make careers out of service in royal administration. The Earl of Mar was a life-long companion of the King's who was an active privy councillor for twenty years before 1603 when he moved with the court to England. He made periodic visits home after that, but in 1617 returned for good, and served as treasurer until 1630. The Earl of Montrose also acted as treasurer during the Arran government and, though suffering a period of disfavour after his fall in 1585, he resumed his council activities, and his place as a lord of session before becoming chancellor in 1599, a post he held until 1604.

Others like Lords Seton, Elphinstone, Fleming, Livingston and Ochiltree failed to reach such high office, but their long years of consistent service in administrative, consultative and executive positions were rewarded with earldoms, lands, or both. A number of these families had been on the wrong side during the Civil War, and for them crown service was a route back to grace and wealth. Certainly some, like the Setons and the Elphinstones, appear to have been very conscious of the prospects royal service could offer, and were fortunate in having brilliant younger sons who added dazzling legal reputations to their noble pedigrees and connections. Thus Lord Seton's and Lord Elphinstone's younger brothers attained higher offices than they did, Alexander Seton becoming James' longest serving Chancellor, and James Elphinstone becoming Secretary of State.

Land, manpower and jurisdictions were, however, the most important measurements of power among the Jacobean nobility, and those lay primarily in the localities. Territorial cohesion was fundamental to such power, and there was a geographical reality to titles like Earl of Argyll, or Earl of Caithness, and to epithets like 'the king of Carrick' in describing the Kennedy Earl of Cassillis. Even the lesser nobility and barons could be closely identified with particular localities. For men like George Gordon, 6th Earl of Huntly, the locality provided a vast power base into which he could retreat when driven from court in 1592, and which quickly recovered from the superficial royal campaigns of the following years. Huntly may have abandoned his Counter-Reformation policies, but in the rebuilding of his sacked castle at Strathbogie he created a magnificent statement of magnate power which defies any suggestion of decline. In an equally defiant manner he also wrote to the King telling him 'none in thir partis mair or vill presum to minister justeis . . . bot we', and in so doing he identified the means by which local power was exercised.

The barony was the basic unit of any locality, and as the hereditary magistrates of the barony courts the Scottish nobility had in their hands a highly effective means of social and political control. As most shrieval, bailie and stewartry courts were also hereditary, and as many of these had regality rights – the right to try and punish offences which were usually within the jurisdiction of the crown – judicial authority was effectively devolved into the hands of the nobility. Acting as landlord and magistrate the nobleman exerted a control over the locality with which the crown could never compete, and when in 1609 justices of the peace were imposed in an effort to reduce private authority, they failed completely.

If feudal structures formed the essential framework on which local power hung, the greater part of its substance was less tangible. Scottish lordship and kinship was much commented upon by the Scots themselves, and by foreign observers. 'In what place in the world will kin, friends and servants adventure more for their lords?' Sir Henry Lee wrote in a letter to Lord Burghley. Such loyalty, with its mutual obligations to protect and to serve, put noblemen at the heads of sprawling networks of friends, kinsmen, dependants, tenants and servants, and formed the sinews of political life at every level.

There, in the surname and in the bonds of manrent and maintenance, the identity of the community was created; there the nobleman was less the feudal lord, and more like the tribal chief, and even the King was referred to as 'my soverane and cheif' by one of his Stewart kinsmen. There was, of course, a dark side to such bonds which was most commonly expressed in the bloody and savage vengeance of the 'barbarous feidis', and in the shielding of criminals from formal justice, such as when Huntly protected John Gordon of Gight because 'he must be a Gordon when it comes to the worst'. Criticism of such behaviour, and the attitudes which underpinned it, was vocal in the church by the end of the sixteenth century, but the process of driving a wedge between the nobility and their followers was a long one which was not completed in the Highlands until the eighteenth century.

The wealth of the Scottish nobility relative to that of other status groups in Scottish society, or in relation to other European aristocracies has never been quantified. Some men certainly were very rich by any standard. George Keith, 5th Earl Marischal who founded Marischal College in Aberdeen in 1593, was one 'lefte very welthye'. Like Marischal, the Hamiltons and the Ruthvens held highly productive lands, but such wealth created enemies and both families were ruined, the Ruthvens permanently. The problem for most noblemen was that so much of their wealth was tied up in land, and much of their income was in kind, thus allowing them to maintain large households and retinues, and to entertain on a lavish scale. However, to purchase luxury articles in the cash economy, and to sustain themselves at court, particularly in London, they had to find credit and pensions.

Before 1603, English, French and Spanish sources were tapped – 'they will do anything for money' wrote one Spanish official – and after the union they were highly successful in plundering the English court. For those who failed to attract sufficient funding, the merciless inflation of the period could exact a high price as credit dried up, the last of their estates were mortgaged, and they faced imprisonment for debt. Lord Berridale spent years in prison for his father's debts, the 7th Earl of Atholl's mismanagement of his affairs was so bad that the privy council intervened to preserve some of the inheritance, and the 12th

Earl of Crawford, 'the prodigal earl', died having lost all his estates, and leaving an only daughter, unmarried and poverty stricken. Walter Scott, 1st Earl of Buccleuch, also was brought close to disaster, but had the sense to stop before it was too late, and to take up service with the States General of Holland in order to avoid his creditors, and to earn a living. Few noble families faced poverty, but the price rise was not unnoticed, and there were few objections, and little snobbery offered when James' new creations brought an influx of new money, and new sources of money into the noble estate.

As was the case elsewhere in Europe, religion divided the Scottish nobility, but in the Jacobean period those divisions cut less deeply than one might expect. No Scottish nobleman died for his faith, and while Catholic revolts did take place, there was great reluctance to draw blood in a society where vengeance could be expected. The two political executions of the period, those of Morton and Gowrie, both left a legacy of feud, including an attempt by the Ruthvens to kill the King. James did demand religious conformity, at least in public, and he wrote to Huntly telling him that his titles and lands would be guaranteed for his sons, but that 'if your conscience be so kittle' that he could not conform, 'look never to be a Scottishman again'. For Huntly and Errol this was too high a price to pay, and they returned from exile to face years of hounding from the reformed kirk. Yet among both their families were to be found priests and nuns, while they themselves continued to provide enough shelter to keep regional Catholicism alive. For the 10th Earl of Angus, who like so many others was converted while visiting France, personal piety came uppermost, and he retired there until his death, having been refused permission to come home and say a 'last guidnicht' to country, kinsmen and friends. A similar commitment was found in the 7th Earl of Argyll who shocked the Protestant establishment in 1617 with his conversion, and his decision to enter Spanish service. The drift back to

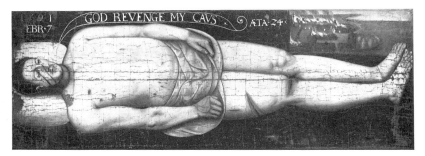

*The body of James Stewart, 2nd Earl of Moray, the 'Bonnie Earl'. Moray was murdered by Huntly at his home at Donibristle in 1592 in the most violent feud of the reign. This portrait was carried in procession by Moray's friends to inspire vengeance.*

Catholicism among the nobility from the 1580s appeared to justify the Jesuit strategy of concentrating on the élite, but they were out-thought and out-worked by a kirk which put its energies into mass teaching and universal discipline.

In spite of that, the church found few noblemen who measured up to its expectations of a godly magistracy. The older generation of Protestant leaders, men like Moray, Argyll, Morton, Glamis and Gowrie, had all died by the early 1580s, mourned for in their passing, but criticised while they lived for refusing to concede to the ministers' financial demands, or to give their backing to the presbyterians. Those who followed were even more disappointing, and only the young Earl of Angus who died in 1588, aged only thirty-three, had the full approval of James Melville, the presbyterian diarist. The premature death of 'Good, godly and stout' Angus, like that of Glamis – a correspondent of Beza's – was a bitter blow to the Protestant clergy, and their efforts to make martyrs out of the murdered Moray and the *politique* Bothwell were shoddy failures.

Measuring religious conviction in any age is always difficult, but one can detect among both Catholic and Protestant noblemen a growing public acceptance of the church's sexual morality, a decline in violent behaviour, and a concern for the religious education of their families. One can describe this as a further step in the Christianisation of a ruling class, as part of the civilising process, or as the acceptance of bourgeois values by the élite, but whatever one calls it, it did contribute to a change in the ethos of the nobility during this period.

Death came for most Scottish noblemen between the ages of forty-five and fifty-five, and there were few who outlived their sixties, the 1st Lord Melville's ninety-four years being a rare exception. Power and responsibility came young for most of them, and at the King's twenty-first birthday in 1587, the average age of the higher nobility was twenty-seven. Just under two hundred men held titles during the period from the end of the Civil War in 1573 and the King's death in 1625, and of these only twelve met violent deaths; five on the scaffold, six in feuds, and one in an English raid. What the majority of the remainder died of one does not really know, nor is there much information about their health. However, Angus died of consumption, the 7th Lord Borthwick of 'the Frenche decease', the 5th Earl of Cassillis died after a horse fell on him, and the 5th Earl of Huntly collapsed in a fatal fit during a game of football. Whatever the reasons, their life expectancy appears to have been little better or worse than comparable status groups elsewhere in Europe.

Almost as common as death was marriage, and only eight men chose to remain bachelors, or died before a marriage could take place. Twenty-one was the average age for a first marriage, which suggests

*J*ames Douglas, Earl of Morton, the fourth and last regent
during the reign of James VI. He was executed in 1581,
accused of having connived at the murder of Darnley.

that a high proportion were arranged by fathers, or tutors, before their
sons, or wards, came of age. Yet the marriage relationship was a stable
one with a mere one in twenty breaking up in divorce, while two-thirds
of the Scottish nobility only ever married once. Where the wife died first
it was common to remarry, and a few went on to a third marriage. The
wives themselves were drawn almost exclusively from the landed class

*John Erskine, 2nd Earl of Mar, who was James' oldest and lifelong friend. Both were brought up at Stirling Castle where Buchanan was their tutor.*

of baronial rank and above, though after 1603 some penetration of the English marriage market did begin.

Around a third of the female children of noblemen married within their own class, and formed the upper end of the market, but the daughters of wealthy barons and lairds could offer equally attractive contracts, and hard-headed business sense, or political considerations overruled any defects in status. Few of these women emerge from their husbands' shadows, but some, like Annas Keith who married the regent Moray and then the 6th Earl of Argyll, and who persistently defied Morton's commands to hand over Queen Mary's jewellery, were impressive individuals in their own right. How well their husbands treated them is unclear, but church and state did frown on marital violence, at least among the nobility, and Lord Borthwick was hauled before the privy council for severely beating his wife. Kinsmen were also protective in a society where agnatic relationships remained so powerful. Up until the establishment of Queen Anne's household in 1590 the Scottish court was essentially a male domain, though some women, like Elizabeth Stewart, whose third husband was Chancellor Arran, did acquire influence and reputations there. However, while a number did spend much of their lives at court, for most noblewomen life was lived at the more mundane level of bearing and rearing children, and assisting in estate management.

Alexander Elphinstone, 4th Lord Elphinstone, and his wife, Jane Livingston, spawned nineteen children between their wedding in 1575 and 1599 when their last child was born. Of those fourteen male and five female children, nine failed to reach adulthood, including six of the last seven, born during the dearth of the 1590s. Of the remainder only two outlived their father, but Lord Elphinstone lived on until 1638 when he was ninety-six. How typical the Elphinstones were is difficult to gauge as infant deaths were not always recorded, and only fifteen noblemen are known to have had more than ten children, often by more than one wife. However, one does know that just under a thousand noble children attained maturity (excluding the low number of known bastards), which means that the average nobleman had to find marriages, lands and careers for between five and six children. While finding husbands for the daughters was not difficult, many lesser men being quite happy to be connected to a noble house even through a younger sister, the sons were less easily provided for. A large proportion of them do not appear to have married, and while around a quarter of them could aspire to titles most ended up as minor lairds on estates set aside by their fathers, and a sizeable minority took up military service on the continent.

Little evidence has survived of what family life was like among the nobility. At one extreme there is the starving to death in Girnigo dungeons of the Master of Caithness by his father, and, on the other hand, one has evidence of affection from letters like that by Lord Maxwell to a friend in which he refers to 'the welfare of my bairnes', especially his favourite, 'My las Elizabeth'. Kinship can be exaggerated, and feuds did exist within the kindred, but the very strong bonds of loyalty which characterised the Scottish family, and the degree of localism in Scottish society, leave an impression of communal love, expressed as kindness – kinship – which challenges the common misconception of a brutalised family life in the pre-modern era.

Far more has been read into the King's almost doubling of the nobility than can be justified. The growth of what was already a large nobility by English standards – Scotland had more peers than England in 1603 – but not perhaps by French or Polish standards, looks more startling than it actually was. Its effects were not to create a new 'noblesse de robe' who were thereafter submissive servants of the crown, but to increase the noble estate in parliament, and inject new wealth and blood into their adopted class. A few struggling noble families might have resented being overtaken in their localities by these new men, but the great magnate families stayed ahead of the field with enhanced titles and even greater rewards. The heads of the Campbell, Gordon, Hamilton and Douglas houses had little to fear from these recruits, many of whom sought the patronage of, and alliance with the older families. Nor was there anything very revolutionary about the social base of these new peers. A number, like the already mentioned Alexander Seton, 1st Earl of Dunfermline, and James Elphinstone, 1st Lord of Balmerino, were younger sons of noblemen, as was Lord Spynie who was recruited through the court rather than through the administration. Many came from among the baronage, and were already chiefs of large and powerful kindreds. Men like Kenneth Mackenzie, 1st Lord Kintail, Walter Scott, 1st Lord Scott, and Alexander Stewart, 1st Lord Garleis, all had the lands, the men and the local offices which made them obvious candidates for a title.

Household service remained as important a route to nobility as it ever had, and Lords Melville and Blantyre received their entitlement after long years as courtiers. More spectacularly George Hume, a gentleman of the bedchamber and master of the King's wardrobe, and David Murray, the King's cup-bearer and master of the royal stables, both acquired a string of titles, offices and rewards, and remained throughout their lives in the inner ring of household men whom the King trusted. Finally, there were those who worked their way up through the legal system to a place in the royal administration. These men were the replacements for the clergy who staffed crown offices before 1560. Some like John Maitland, Lord Thirlstane, came from well established legal dynasties, but the most successful of them all, Thomas Hamilton, was a younger son of a less well established family who worked to become the best advocate of his day, was appointed Lord Advocate, and went on to an earldom, a succession of offices under James and Charles, and was worth a fortune at his death. Yet whatever their origins, these men, and their heirs, adopted the lifestyles, attitudes and values of a nobility whose own habits and beliefs were changing as they became better educated, and as they freed themselves from the need to be evaluated primarily for their military prowess. This combination of adaptation and recruitment resulted in a stronger nobility, more equipped to hold on to its power and its privileges, and to remain the dominant class in Scotland.

# CHAPTER VI

# The Scottish Early Modern Burgh

MICHAEL LYNCH

T he urban history of sixteenth- and seventeenth-century Scotland
is in a sense a tale of two cities – Edinburgh and Glasgow. The
merchant princes of Edinburgh – like William Birnie who died in the
Netherlands staple port of Veere in 1569 leaving over £29,000 Scots
(about £6,500 sterling) or William MacMoran, the richest merchant of
his generation, with shares in nine ships and a fortune of over £37,000
Scots (by then worth £3,000 sterling) when he was shot dead by an
Edinburgh schoolboy in 1596 – have been described as the success
story of sixteenth-century Scotland. Theirs was the platform for the
more spectacular fortunes of Edinburgh merchants early in the following
century – like the monopolist and manufacturer Patrick Wood, whose
testament inventory of 1638 revealed investments worth £100,000 Scots
in shipping, salt-panning, manufactories like rope works and trading
ventures stretching from the Baltic to the Canaries but also debts to
match; or like the *doyen* of the mercantile establishment, William Dick
of Braid, who lent and lost over £130,000 Scots to the cause of the
Covenant.

Glasgow has been called by T.C. Smout the boom-town of seventeenth-century Scotland. In 1556 it was only eleventh in the ranking
list of burghs paying national taxation. By 1594 it was fifth, by 1649
fourth and by 1660 second only to Edinburgh. By the Union of 1707
Glasgow had consolidated this position, paying four times as much tax
as its nearest rival, Aberdeen. The rise of Glasgow in the seventeenth
century was all the more spectacular because many of its rivals, like
Dundee and Perth, went into relative if not absolute decline after the
Restoration as they began to lose out to new patterns of trade with
Spain and the Americas as well as to the concentration of the old east-
coast trading routes – to the Baltic, Netherlands and France – on
Edinburgh's port of Leith.

The platform for Glasgow's growing prosperity was established by the
third quarter of the century in a range of manufactories – cloth and linen
works, soap boiling and sugar refining – many of which were organised
in the form of joint stock companies. It is remarkable that one of the
major investors in Glasgow's largest manufactory, which employed 1,400
in the making of cloth, was the principal of the university, William

*The Common Seal of the Burgh of Glasgow, 1605,
marking the new burgh constitution giving opportunities to
craftsmen as well as merchants.*

Dunlop. One reason for Glasgow's phenomenal rise was, so Professor Smout argued, a freer atmosphere which avoided the habitual political bickerings of merchants and craftsmen elsewhere in urban Scotland and escaped the restrictive trade practices and demarcation disputes which elsewhere remained a legacy of the still potent medieval guild system. A second reason – and one less easy to dispute – was the building of a new port, 'the Piraeus of Glasgow', further down the Clyde estuary in 1667. There had been 'new towns' in Scotland before but not new ports like Port Glasgow, which solved the two problems of jurisdiction and access which had plagued other burghs. Edinburgh had taken three centuries after its confirming charter of 1329 to gain undisputed control over its port; the silting of the River Tay had slowly strangled Perth's overseas trade and passed the advantage to its rival at the mouth of the river – Dundee.

Yet there lie behind these generalisations two unresolved sets of assumptions, about both the nature of Scottish urban society and its place in the broader context of the Scottish society and economy as a whole. The serious study of seventeenth-century Glasgow, begun by Professor Smout in a series of articles written in the 1960s, has encouraged a subsequent concentration – by historical geographers as well as economic historians – on the 'pre-industrial town' in Scotland. The Glasgow entrepreneurs of the Restoration period were the forerunners of the famous Glasgow tobacco lords of the eighteenth century. The very notion of the 'pre-industrial town', used with quite unselfconscious regularity in the recent volume of essays *Scottish Urban History*, edited by two historical geographers, George Gordon and Brian Dicks (Aberdeen University Press, 1983), concentrates attention on the rapid abandonment at some point – and in Scotland this is usually in the last quarter of the seventeenth century or the early eighteenth – of the restrictive features in the institutions and structure of the Scottish medieval burgh.

In the wider context of the seventeenth-century economy it is wholly characteristic that the recently published volume five of the *New History of Scotland* series which covers this period begins its detailed treatment of the economy in a separate chapter which opens in 1660. The rise of Glasgow has been developed into a notion of urban take-off; the problem of change has become more fashionable for the seventeenth-century historian than the problem of continuity. A clear indicator of this trend is the curious fact that in Scotland the phrase, 'the early modern town', has scarcely reached the currency of historiography. What is needed to balance the excesses of 'pre-industrial town' history is a more careful examination of how in the early modern period the distinctive structure and institutions of the Scottish medieval burgh were subjected to increasing pressure as a result of various changes, not least of them a rise in urban population in most of the larger towns. The question has yet to be answered – whatever happened to the medieval burgh in Scotland? The question is all the more important to answer because it has to be asked of the century and a half before 1660 which encompassed the Reformation, the Wars of the Covenant, eightfold price inflation and a new and ever-increasing burden of national taxation as well as increasing interference by both the crown and local landowners in the affairs of the burgh.

It is difficult to be certain of the population of many Scottish burghs before the evidence of hearth and poll taxes in the 1690s. Even Glasgow's increase in the seventeenth century is difficult to quantify. Yet there are indications of a significant rise in the population of some of the larger burghs in the sixteenth century. The most precise figures are those for Edinburgh, which had, according to the French visitor Froissart, some 400 houses in 1400. By 1592 when the local kirk session made a census of the burgh it had, despite a recent serious outbreak of plague, 2,239 households which contained 8,003 persons of communicable age (over the age of fourteen). By 1635, when an exhaustive survey was made to assess individual contributions to pay for the burgh's six ministers, Edinburgh had no less than 3,901 households and 903 businesses within the 140 acres bounded by its walls. Outside the walls – in the suburbs clustered at each of the six city gates (clearly portrayed in Gordon of

Rothiemay's remarkably detailed map of 1647), in the adjoining burgh of the Canongate, now the eastern end of the 'Royal Mile', and in the port of Leith two miles away – there were at least 10,000 more inhabitants. The burgh itself had a population of well over 20,000 – the average size of the Scottish urban household is still a matter of guesswork but in some larger towns it may have been in excess of the figure of 4.7 often used from English examples – and greater Edinburgh had over 30,000. Either figure would make Edinburgh more than three times the size of Glasgow throughout the century and larger than contemporary Norwich or Bristol, the largest cities in seventeenth-century England outside London.

The rise of Edinburgh in the sixteenth and seventeenth centuries was symbolised in the soaring tenements of the Lawnmarket at the head of the High Street, of four, five and six storeys and eventually of up to fourteen – among them Gladstone's Land, built *circa* 1620 and now owned by the National Trust for Scotland. The urban tenement, which had been a distinctive feature of the Scottish burgh from an early point in its history, was being stretched to extreme lengths to accommodate the capital's rapidly growing population. The result was that, as one English visitor reported, there were almost as many landlords as there were storeys of tenements. The number of households in the two southern quarters, between the High Street and the old Flodden Wall, doubled between the 1590s and the 1630s. In much the same way the traditional institutions and customs of burgh life were stretched to accommodate the pressures which the early modern period brought to bear upon them.

One of the most serious of these problems was the provision the burgh made for the souls of its inhabitants. From their very beginnings the Scottish burghs had been and remained single parish communities. The names of many burgh churches – St John's, St Mary's, St Nicholas' – reflected the new status given to a community by its simultaneous elevation in the twelfth or thirteenth centuries into the status of a separate parish and royal burgh. The growing demands of piety and the development in the later fifteenth century of separate and incorporated guilds had been met by the elevation of many burgh churches into collegiate status, with separate altars for each of the burgh's guilds. Edinburgh had fourteen incorporated craft guilds as well as a merchant guildry and its parish church of St Giles had more than forty side altars as a result. Yet Scottish Protestantism, in promising a simpler, more direct – as well as a cheaper – faith, posed for itself a severe problem.

Protestantism was, even at its moment of victory in 1560, a minority religion in most Scottish towns – with the possible exception of Perth and Dundee. There were neither enough ministers nor enough urban enthusiasts to make headway quickly. John Knox had one reader to assist him minister to 12,000 souls. It was hardly surprising that only 1,300, less than a fifth of the adult population of the capital, chose to take communion by the new Protestant rite at Easter 1561 – fully eight months after Scotland's official adoption of Protestantism by the Reformation parliament. Knox was joined by a second minister in 1562 but Edinburgh and Dundee were the only Scottish burghs to have more than one minister in the Reformation generation.

It has been pointed out by Patrick Collinson how ineffective one London vicar felt himself to be in the 1630s with a congregation of 1,400 adult parishioners. He would have been considered well off in almost any of the Scottish towns, including the capital. The minister of the small Fife burgh of Culross complained in about 1600 of the 'intolerable burden' of 2,000 communicants. Perth is often thought of as one of the most forward of the Scottish towns in the strength and breadth of its Protestant opinions. Yet it did not appoint a second minister until 1595 and it was only then that the kirk session could institute a system of weekly catechising in place of the perfunctory annual examination of parishioners before communion which had obtained since 1560. There was no magical mass conversion to Protestantism in Edinburgh or elsewhere in urban Scotland. It was not until the 1580s – fully a generation after the Reformation crisis of 1559–60 – that there were signs of real Protestant populist enthusiasm in any of the towns.

The problems posed by the shortage of clerical manpower were overcome only gradually. The Edinburgh census of 1592 was designed by the presbytery to pave the way for the splitting up of the single

*A view of Edinburgh from the Castle battlements.*

parish of St Giles – whose parishioners had since the 1560s worshipped in four different places according to the quarter of the burgh in which they lived. The scheme was to create eight model parishes, each with its own minister and a thousand adult communicants, but practicalities intervened and the eight parishes gave way to four in 1598 and to six in 1641. Glasgow followed suit when its parish was divided into four in 1648 and into six in 1701. If it can be said that there was one point at which the medieval burgh came to an end it was this – the severing of the historic link between burgh community and parish. In England, curiously enough, a mirror image of this process was taking place as boroughs like Exeter, Ipswich and Colchester were forced, at the end of the sixteenth century, to rationalise their anachronistic medieval legacy, not of one parish church but of too many – in Exeter's case nineteen. In this respect as in many others the shape of the urban community was very different in Scotland from what it was in England.

John Knox in his tract of 1558, *A letter addressed to the Commonalty of Scotland*, had forecast that when the new godly society was established rich and poor would both share in it and contribute to it equally. The full consequences of Knox's manifesto did not become clear until five years later when the Edinburgh town council took the unprecedented step of imposing a compulsory household tax of four shillings a year on all inhabitants to pay for the burgh's ministers. This was the first of eight separate fund-raising schemes devised in Edinburgh in the course of the 1560s to pay for the programme of the kirk; some attempted to include poor relief and education alongside payment of the ministry and various degrees of coercion were used.

All schemes foundered. The new religious establishment in Edinburgh was not placed on a stable financial basis until at least the 1580s, perhaps not until the 1630s. The new church was chronically underendowed both in rural and urban Scotland. But most Scottish towns were unaccustomed to direct taxation before the crown made regular demands of them from the 1580s onwards. The Scottish burgess proved remarkably tight-fisted when it came to meeting the bill for the kirk's programme.

Even more remarkable was the entrenched opposition to the establishment of a compulsory poor rate, despite at least a fourfold increase in general prices between 1550 and 1625, growing urban populations and frequent incidence of the plague up to the 1640s. There was no tradition in Scotland of merchant charity to fall back on and there proved to be substantial resistance, in Edinburgh and elsewhere, to a poor rate. In 1575 an act was passed by the Scottish parliament, probably at the prompting of Edinburgh, to enable town councils to raise a compulsory poor rate. The act was in frank imitation of the English parliamentary legislation of 1572. Yet there was a vital difference. The legislation of Elizabethan parliaments on poor relief built on relatively successful measures which

*Braun and Hogenberg's Map of Edinburgh 1582.*

had already been taken in certain towns like Norwich, where elaborate machinery designed to rationalise the treatment of its poor had come into effect in 1571. In England parliamentary legislation sought to extend a system already in existence. In Scotland the act of 1575 was designed to give added force to a system which had already been tried a number of times in Edinburgh and resisted.

When implemented in Edinburgh the new compulsory poor rate ironically raised less than the old *ad hoc* system of voluntary donations at the church door on Sundays. It lasted less than two years, ending in acrimony between town council and kirk session, each blaming the other for the fact that the town had proved unwilling to accept direct taxation even to support its own poor. Scotland muddled on into the seventeenth century with a voluntary system and the unpalatable problem of the poor was passed from civil authority to the kirk session

Who were the victims of the point-blank refusal of urban estab-lishments to accept a compulsory poor rate? The three-quarters of a century after 1550 was a period of sharply rising prices, recurrent though usually localised food shortages as well as rising population. Yet there was oddly little social unrest in early modern Scotland. There were no peasant uprisings in the countryside and no bread riots in the towns. There were, instead, fairly frequent minor riots in some of the larger towns involving the producers of bread and other basic commodities in protest against town councils which deliberately held down the prices of foodstuffs to artificially low levels. The Dundee bakers even took the town council to the Court of Session, the highest civil court in the land, in 1561. The rulers of the Scottish burghs used a cheap food policy – with apparent success – as an alternative to a properly organised system of poor relief.

The burgh of Perth, where John Knox incited the 'rascal multitude' to loot the friaries in 1559, which proved the flashpoint of the Reformation movement, seems to have experienced an unusual amount of social tension. It proved to be fertile ground for populist anticlericalism. Yet in other towns there was little sign that the urban Reformation was anything other than a respectable bourgeois revolution which confirmed power in traditional hands. Knox himself refused to be drawn into a fleshers' riot in Edinburgh only eighteen months later. When a Protestant subscription list was drawn up in the capital in 1562 it was dominated by the lawyers, larger merchants and a craft aristocracy drawn from the wealthier guilds like goldsmiths and tailors. The words of the document encapsulate the spirit of the first generation of urban Protestantism: 'Not doubting but who freely and gladly give to this godly work God shall abundantly increase his substance and bless the same'.

The militant tendency in urban Protestantism first emerged fully a generation after the Reformation of 1559–60. By the early 1580s there was a new grass-roots presbyterian enthusiasm in some of the towns, taking its name if not all its inspiration from Andrew Melville. The Reformation and its repercussions had largely been debated within the privileged confines of the town council-chamber or the kirk session. The debates of the Melvillian period were conducted in a much wider forum and had potentially serious social overtones. There were signs of kirk sessions splitting along the lines of wealthy élitist elders against deacons, mostly *nouveaux* Calvinists from humbler social origins. By the early seventeenth century these 'giddy-headed' radicals were expert in reciting passages from Scripture and tossing bibles at their own ministers in kirk session meetings. By 1618, with James VI's attempts to introduce into the kirk quasi-Anglican liturgical practices such as kneeling at communion, a new-style urban Calvinist, fuelled by inner conviction verging on antinomianism as much as by political animus, had appeared. Scripture or the individual conscience was brought into play not only against what was seen as a corrupt Erastian church and its ministers but also the urban establishment itself. When the provost of Edinburgh could bluntly be told by an obscure deacon in the kirk session, 'Sir, You are but a sessioner here', the challenge could not go unheeded. Procedural devices were brought into play from 1618 onwards to flood the kirk session with safe, establishment figures.

In other respects what tensions there were in burgh society were successfully muted by the expedient of selective recruitment into the urban establishment. Burgh historians have begun to cast doubt on the old orthodoxy that the Scottish burgh was from about 1470 onwards convulsed by sharpening tension between merchants and craftsmen. There was in most small towns almost no sign of this and in the larger towns like Perth and Edinburgh craftsmen were admitted in large numbers to the merchant guildry. In doing so these craftsmen became not merchants but craft employers who in the process gained more power, both in burgh affairs and over their fellow craftsmen. A craft aristocracy – of tailors, goldsmiths, skinners, surgeons – was emerging in the larger towns like Edinburgh and Perth in the course of the sixteenth century and the burgh oligarchy was being widened to accommodate it. Yet if the merchant guildry was not as narrow an enclave of privilege as has hitherto been thought, was Glasgow so very different? The notion that seventeenth-century Glasgow rose because it enjoyed an atmosphere free of merchant-craft rivalries may prove to have been founded on shifting sands.

A fundamental reappraisal of the changing balance of power between centre and localities in early modern Scotland is in progress, stimulated by the appearance of Jenny Wormald's volume in the *New History of Scotland* series. This new revisionism needs also to be applied to the towns. The Scottish burghs had for centuries operated within what were a remarkably loose set of reins for a feudal kingdom. Those reins were hauled in sharply in the course of the sixteenth century and especially during the personal reign of James VI. The tax net was cast more widely over the burgh population to meet the crown's new fiscal demands. There were political repercussions too.

It had long been royal practice to plant favourites as provosts of burghs. Now whole town councils and even kirk sessions were nominated, as in Edinburgh and Perth in 1584. Yet, curiously, other burghs – like Dundee and Aberdeen – escaped with only an occasional cursory royal visit. What was also relevant to this new but selective royal interventionist policy was the fact that since the mid-fifteenth century a number of burghs had drifted into the patronage networks of local nobles or lairds. In Perth the two patterns met head on when the local noble family of the Earls of Gowrie fell out with the crown in 1584; for the next fifteen years successive court and country factions fell in and out of power on the town council. The late sixteenth century witnessed the return in a number of different ways of the royal burghs to the national stage and their closer involvement with central government. That journey – and the different demands it made on burgh politics and finances – had more effect than any other factor in hastening the process of the reshaping of the medieval burgh.

# CHAPTER VII

# Reformation and Revolution, Kirk and Crown 1560–1690

JAMES KIRK

In no less than four major crises between 1560 and 1690, disaffected Scots succeeded in pushing ahead, in wholly unprecedented fashion, with far-reaching constitutional and ecclesiastical reform in defiance of the wishes of the crown. The first decisive break came with the Reformation which in Scotland, unlike in England, took the form of a rebellion not simply against Rome but also against the constituted government of the realm. Resorting to arms, the Protestant 'Lords of the Congregation' in 1559 deposed from the regency the Queen Mother, Mary of Guise, who ruled in the name of her absent daughter, Queen Mary, who then was also Queen of France, and sought to transfer power to a provisional government of their own choosing, dominated by Protestant lords. The Protestant victory of 1560 severed not merely the links with Rome but also Scotland's traditional alliance with France by effecting a diplomatic realignment away from largely Catholic France towards friendship with the Protestant England of Queen Elizabeth, whose military intervention in Scotland had largely secured the successful outcome of the Reformation. Cultural and educational ties with France were less readily dissolved, but the newly established 'amity' with England, which no subsequent Scottish government was ever to repudiate, far less to relinquish, had powerful long-term effects on the Scottish kirk and nation.

A second turning-point, dramatic in itself and decisive enough in its consequences, emerged in 1567 when a faction of nobles, the confederate lords, took to arms in opposing Mary's impetuous marriage to Bothwell, a man widely suspected as the murderer of her second husband, Darnley. Ostensibly, their action was to free Mary from Bothwell's domination and to defend her son, Prince James, but in reality, as the rival armies faced each other on the field, Mary's surrender to her opponents resulted in her imprisonment on Lochleven and in her enforced abdication in favour of her son, with Moray, her Protestant half-brother, acting as regent. In a bid to justify the deposition of their Queen, Moray and his associates subsequently contended that, by her exercise of a 'cruel tyranny', the estates of the realm had found Mary 'unworthy to reign', but all this was retrospective and very special pleading. Indeed, it is worth recalling that throughout the Middle Ages no previous Scottish monarch had met such a fate at the hands of subjects. Two earlier Stewart kings, it is true, had died violently at the hands of assassins; and much earlier King John had been deposed in 1296, not indeed by his own subjects but by Edward I of England.

The novelty of the action taken in 1567 needs stressing. There was simply no Scottish precedent for Mary's deposition. Never before had Scottish opponents of the regime taken the drastic and highly unusual step of, first, capturing the monarch, then extracting a compulsory abdication and, finally, recognising the heir to the throne as king while the deposed sovereign still lived. But those who provided the religious justification for the Reformation-rebellion in 1559 were no less ready in 1567 to assert the constitutional right of subjects to correct their prince and even to depose a 'tyrant'. The revolution of 1567, therefore, amounted to far more than a mere palace *coup*. But it also proved divisive by splitting public opinion. Support for Mary and for James, which led to six years of intermittent civil warfare, cut right across the religious issue. Yet there could be no mistaking the fact that the thirteen-month-old James who in 1566 had been baptised with Catholic rites, at Mary's insistence, was crowned at a Protestant service in 1567; and his upbringing as a Protestant prince seemed assured under a succession of regents committed to the reformed cause and to friendship with England.

The eventual stability provided by James' exceptionally long reign spanning fifty-eight years brought the country peace and a measure of prosperity unwitnessed for a generation. Yet the personal union of the crowns in 1603, when James VI went south to occupy the English throne, raised in fresh and more urgent form a host of complex constitutional and religious problems which James ultimately failed to resolve and so bequeathed a bitter legacy to Charles I. The union in one person of two separate crowns in two very different kingdoms, each with its distinctive legislative, administrative and ecclesiastical traditions, strictly speaking, amounted to no more than each realm sharing the same sovereign; but, in practice, James' increasingly overbearing and autocratic attitude towards the affairs in his northern kingdom, and especially his cherished if misguided policy of forcing the Scottish kirk into ever closer conformity with her sister church in England, needlessly antagonised Scottish sentiment. James, however, was safe so long as his triple alliance of king, nobles and bishops held together. Charles, at best an imperfect politician, stood in jeopardy, for his well-intentioned but ineptly executed schemes antagonised even his best friends, forcing together the highly dangerous combination of alienated nobles and disgruntled presbyterian ministers, the two potentially explosive elements which James, mindful of the lessons of the Reformation, had taken great care to keep apart.

In the next confrontation, ecclesiastical discontent with the whole drift of the King's insensitive policy of remoulding the kirk on increasingly English lines combined with widespread constitutional grievances at Charles' exercise of prerogative powers, his high-handed and arbitrary treatment of council and parliament, his apparent disregard for the liberties of the subject and for the rights of property, which his ill-conceived Act of Revocation had threatened to sweep aside. All this found forceful expression in the National Covenant of 1638, a cleverly contrived document, couched in legal and constitutional terms, superficially conservative in tone, and designed as a religious band (or bond of union) – justifiably so since the King in 1634 had construed legitimate petitioning as treasonable – but which nonetheless called for two radical and far-reaching reforms which, if granted, would turn the government of Scotland on its head: the right to hold 'free' parliaments and 'free' general assemblies of the church, unfettered by royal manipulation. The Covenant also spelt out to Charles, as well as to everyone else, that the King was bound by, and could not override, the fundamental laws of the realm.

Such an appeal to the constitutional rights of general assemblies and parliaments in determining and approving appropriate policies in church and state was wholly incompatible with the exalted conception of the powers of the crown and divine-right monarchy which Charles wholeheartedly espoused. What had really failed was Charles' whole system of government. He had succeeded almost in uniting the nation against his policies. As a consequence, his authority in Scotland collapsed. Not only had the opposition already created a rival administration in Edinburgh, forcing the privy council to retreat to Linlithgow, but each side also showed a readiness to resort to force to impose its will upon the nation. As King and Covenanters made military preparations, the prospects for a peaceful settlement looked far from bright.

Concessions granted by a King who was merely playing for time and whom his opponents could no longer trust merely stiffened the Covenanters' resolve to press ahead with more radical moves to undo the whole apparatus of royal changes effected in the church. Once this was speedily achieved, attention focused on imposing wide-ranging restraints or limitations designed to curtail the powers of the crown. This experiment in limited constitutional monarchy, which parliament was intent on carrying through in 1640, aimed at replacing the arbitrary exercise of prerogative powers with a form of representative and responsible government. All in all, the measures passed amounted to little short of a constitutional revolution effected, as it was, during the brief interlude between the First and Second Bishops' Wars in complete defiance of the wishes of the crown. And more was to come in 1641 when the Covenanters asserted parliamentary control over the executive

*M*ary Queen of Scots and her son James, 1583; by an
unknown artist. In fact, Mary and her son never met after her
flight to England in 1567; this painting may well have
prompted Mary's Catholic allies to canvass support for her
return to the throne of Scotland as joint sovereign with her son.

and judiciary, again achieved at the crown's expense; and Charles himself was forced to recognise this novel constitution, which he so much
despised, and thereby to grant it full legal sanction.

Such drastic reform of the constitution in church and state was soon
to be overtaken by events and proved short-lived. The increasingly
revolutionary tendencies exhibited by the more extreme Covenanters
led by Argyll alienated more moderate adherents like Montrose who
argued that the liberties of the subject and the prerogative powers of the
crown were complementary, not contradictory, and that the ideals of the
Covenant were in danger of distortion by extremists intent on depriving
the King of all power, so paving the way for the onset of dictatorship.
Further dissensions arose not least as a result of Scottish participation
in the English Civil War through an alliance, the Solemn League and
Covenant, with the English parliamentarians. This, in turn, led to civil
war in Scotland with the emergence of a royalist party under Montrose,
pledged to support the King who, on surrendering to the Scots in 1646,
had been handed over to the English parliamentarians for his refusal to
accept the Covenants. The ominous split among the Covenanters, and
the seizure of power by theocratic extremists in 1648, ultimately had the

85

*The Arch-Prelate of St Andrews comes under attack whilst reading from the Revised Prayer Book for Scotland in St Giles Cathedral in Edinburgh in 1637.*

effect of delivering Scotland almost on a plate to Oliver Cromwell. The ensuing conquest gave rise to an enforced though fleeting union with England, conceived on not ungenerous terms but noticeably lacking in popular support.

Yet the widely welcomed Restoration of the monarchy in 1660, which had its antecedents in England – though the Scottish estates had already recognised Charles II as King in 1650 – also restored many of the vexed and unresolved problems in church and state which had generated so much strife and bitterness in the past and which augured ill for the new regime. Once Charles had been restored on terms in England, it was too late for the Scots to look for concessions. By sweeping aside the constitutional and presbyterian reforms of the 1640s, the settlement at one stroke undid the work of the Covenanters. The return of episcopacy and the prerogative powers of the crown were but two aspects of a many-sided conservative reaction against the political, ecclesiastical and, in some senses, social radicalism of the 1640s and 1650s. At all costs, royal authority had now to be safeguarded. Yet the repressive policies of the regime towards any expression of dissent, which goaded the peasantry of the south-west to rise in protest in 1666, reveal the new heights to which arbitrary rule was pushed, for the men who took part in the Pentland rising ought not to be too hastily dismissed as half-mad religious fanatics; they saw themselves as fairly moderate men deprived of legitimate constitutional means for redressing their grievances. Once more, the 'Whigs', or more radical Covenanters, took to questioning the rights and powers of bishops and, inevitably, those of the King who sustained them. But the brief glimmerings of something like a parliamentary opposition, demanding a redress of grievances in 1673,

were soon suppressed, if not wholly extinguished, when Charles swift-
ly dissolved the meeting and postponed calling a further parliament till
1681. Within the country at large, neither the oscillating policies of
conciliation nor renewed repression redeemed a deteriorating situation
for the government which looked as if it had lost its grasp. On the heels
of this came the ominous tendencies following James' accession in 1685
which highlighted the extreme importance which the new King attached
to his prerogative powers and which seemed to sweep aside the force of
existing statute law. His tampering with the constitution in a wholly
unacceptable manner, together with his undermining of the established
episcopal church by his professed toleration in an effort to alleviate his
loyal Catholic subjects from the full rigours of the penal laws, all helped
to precipitate his downfall.

But again, when revolution came, the initiative is to be found
not in Scotland, where no solid core of organised opposition had
yet emerged, but in England, as Shaftesbury and the Whigs turned
to William. Thereafter, James' flight to France enabled the English
to invent the comfortable fiction that, by his departure, James had
abdicated. Yet a very different line was taken in Scotland where
frustrated constitutionalists were presented with an unexpected opportunity to overhaul and reform the constitution. This was given tangible
expression not least in the Claim of Right which asserted not that James
had abdicated but that, by his transgressions, he had forfeited his right to
the throne of his northern kingdom. Implicit in this claim was the recognition that the monarchy was understood to be contractual. This strand
of thought is traceable in cogent form at least as far back as the Scottish
Reformation itself, and its expression owed much to the earlier views of
Knox and Buchanan when they sought to justify the rebellions of 1559
and 1567. Nor were the reforms of the 1640s entirely overlooked in the
settlement of 1689–90, for once again the powers of the crown in church
and state were significantly reduced, though in less drastic fashion than
that attempted in 1641, and presbyterianism finally replaced episcopacy
as the established form of church government in Scotland.

The century or so from Reformation to Revolution forms a natural unity; and in many ways the issues arising from the Reformation
hold the key to the unfolding pattern of events which lay ahead. The
impulses triggered off by the Reformation continued to reverberate,
with unsettling consequences for kings and people, for generations to
come. The forces producing the Reformation, in short, unlocked a
veritable Pandora's box which no monarch thereafter ever managed
fully to secure. Even the Reformation itself presents something of a
puzzle. Some recent writings suggest that Protestantism as a popular
movement was non-existent and that it was merely the coincidence of
political dissatisfaction among nobles and the religious radicalism of a

few preachers which sparked off the Reformation-rebellion of 1559. But such a tidy and oversimplified evaluation may safely be set aside as at odds with the evidence. As Professor Gordon Donaldson's study *All the Queen's Men* (1983) has demonstrated in a brief but cogent treatment of the subject:

> Protestantism had a firm footing in Scotland long before a parliament met in 1560 to abolish papal authority and forbid the celebration of the Latin mass. Some recent assessments have underestimated the strength of the attachment to the cause of reform and have even suggested that when the religious change was officially made it was no more than a matter of manipulation for political reasons. This reinterpretation is not merely the result of one of those changes of fashion which periodically afflict historical writing. The fact is that in the later twentieth century concepts of moral guilt are at a discount and the doctrine of sin has become unfashionable . . . Thus few now have any appreciation of the despair of those who admit to being 'miserable sinners' and the solace which they can find in the Passion of Christ. It was not so in the sixteenth century.

After a thorough and refreshing review of the evidence, Professor Donaldson concludes:

> The notion that the Reformation was not a popular movement, but something carried through by a clique of nobles making religion a cloak for their own selfish ends and in defiance of majority opinion, and that Protestantism took root only after a parliament had legislated in its favour, cannot be entertained.

All this needs saying, for it is hard to see how the weight of evidence, much of it long available in print, can be so blithely disregarded except by the adoption of an ostrich-like posture. Indeed, in the more politically influential parts of the realm, it was precisely the popular appeal of Protestantism, which arose from beneath to claim power rather than be imposed from the top, which made it impossible thereafter for either crown or nobility adequately to temper the pace and direction which the new church, so uncompromisingly, had charted for itself. At best, politics only help explain the timing of the Reformation, and its successful outcome, but not its *raison d'être*, which has to be sought elsewhere. Again, some recent writers have cast such doubt on the actions and motives of the reformers that it becomes increasingly hard to see how anything of consequence was ever achieved. But decisive action undoubtedly followed.

The Revolution of 1560, with startling success, had challenged and overthrown the church which once had commanded the devotion of the nation but which, when faced with collapse, showed little inclination in rallying to recover the lost ground. The work of the Reformation parliament in 1560, though denied royal sanction, was short and swift. Concentrating on essentials, it cut the ground from beneath the old order by abolishing the mass and papal jurisdiction, and substituting a Protestant Confession of Faith. This done, parliament assigned to others the details of working out the nature of the changes. All in all, the Scots found no need for the ponderous and protracted deliberations which had characterised the Henrician Reformation parliament from 1529 to 1536, which severed the English church from the papacy by subjecting it to the control of the crown in parliament. In Scotland, whose Catholic Queen was still in France, the new kirk was accorded that rare and exhilarating experience, denied to most churches, of determining its own programme and constitution; and its cherished independence, which political circumstances permitted it to achieve, was not lightly to be lost.

The radical approach of the new church, which marked a decisive break with the past, is (and was) apparent for all to see. In doctrine, the characteristic Protestant emphasis on original sin, atonement, justification by faith alone, predestination and the verbal inspiration of scripture found homely expression in the Scots Confession of Faith which, with the First Book of Discipline, rejected transubstantiation and replaced the seven sacraments of the old church by two: baptism and the Lord's Supper. In worship, out went Latinity, sacerdotalism, altars and unleavened wafers, auricular confession, the cult of Mary and the saints, holy days and feast days, prayers for the dead, belief in purgatory, the use of responses, the sign of the cross, crucifixes, images and elaborate ritual, surplices, or choir dress, and eucharistic vestments, organs and choristers, the plainsong of great churches and the silence of poor churches. In came a simple service based on preaching, bible study, prayers and the metrical psalms sung to common tunes, and with this the active participation of the people who, no longer passive spectators, were encouraged to sing God's praise and to receive both wine and bread at communion, seated corporately at tables. The new responsibility assumed by the congregation was channelled in other directions too, not least in the role assigned to them in the courts of the new church, and, again, in the recognition that their consent was necessary in selecting their minister and in appointing from their ranks elders and deacons to assist in running parish affairs.

In discipline, the penitential system of the medieval church was jettisoned; so too its judicial courts and legislative councils and, with their disappearance, the displacement of the corpus of canon law. In their place, the new church set up its own concentric series of courts, linking the localities with the church's general assembly at the centre in wholly unprecedented fashion. In establishing its own reformed ministry and distinctive system of government, the kirk with equal resolution in 1560 rejected the ancient system of benefices and with it all hierarchical titles from acolyte to archbishop. Here was no mere tinkering with the ecclesiastical edifice. It was designed as a radical, root-and-branch reformation; and, seeking its inspiration from the examples of 'the best reformed churches' overseas, it went much further than the moderate and tempered reforms in England. Again, much of this new structure came into being, and more besides this was achieved, without tarrying for the magistrate's permission. One recent writer, who remarked that in Scotland 'only the civil magistrate possessed the power of excommunication', could scarcely have displayed a greater misunderstanding of Scottish reformed practice, where the kirk in exercising the right to excommunicate without 'tarrying for the magistrate' won a victory which even Calvin failed fully to secure in Geneva.

This tradition of ecclesiastical independence which thus emerged (and with it the kirk's disinclination to accept royal supremacy over it, even with the accession of a Protestant prince in 1567) found early expression in the doctrine of the two kingdoms, to which Scottish reformers resorted as early as 1559, and for which, of course, ample continental precedents could be found in that strand of reformed thought traceable from Beza and Calvin back to Bucer and Oecolampadius, and, in some senses, to Luther himself. The historians' claim, so assiduously cultivated, that the 'two kingdoms' theory was a later innovation of the 1570s, supplied by the presbyterian Andrew Melville and the Second Book of Discipline, can therefore safely be rejected as at variance with the facts of history.

Attempts by successive governments to curb the kirk's independence took different forms and met with varying success. Queen Mary's claims in the early 1560s that the church's general assembly, which met where and when it chose without royal licence, amounted to an illegal convocation of the lieges were reiterated by the Regent Morton in the 1570s but were effectively countered by the church's assertion that its assembly existed by divine right. The tempting financial bait of advancing ministers, as the crown's nominees, to the old pre-reformation bishoprics, so recognised in 1572, was designed to pave the way for the emergence of a Protestant episcopate and thereby a ready means for advancing royal influence in the church, but the scheme was repudiated by the general assembly soon afterwards and the crown failed to achieve its objectives. Yet the issue remained contentious since the crown had a trump card up its sleeve in appointing titular bishops who would have access to the revenues of the bishoprics and who, while playing no part in ecclesiastical administration, would nevertheless vote in parliament as bishops and be eligible for election to the privy council. By 1584, the crown in parliament felt sufficiently confident to assert its authority

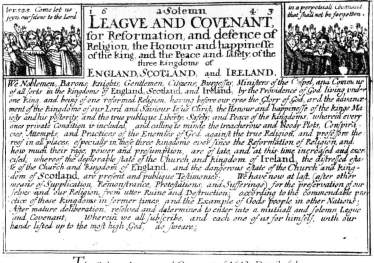

*The Solemn League and Covenant of 1643. Detail of the engraving by Hollar.*

by proscribing presbyterianism, reintroducing episcopacy and asserting royal supremacy over the church. Even so, the victory was short-lived; and by 1592 the crown was forced to acknowledge the defeat it sustained in the intervening years and assent to a statute recognising the church's presbyterian constitution.

Beneath the controversial issue of whether or not the church should be governed by bishops or by a system of courts, in which the presbytery provided a cohesive link between localities and the centre, lay the vexed question of the relationship between church and state, or between political and ecclesiastical authority. The general assembly's distaste for any settlement which smacked of blatant erastianism had been evident from the outset. Not only did it claim that prince and civil magistrate were subject to ecclesiastical censure and, if need be, to excommunication, but it earnestly strove to inculcate a belief in a strictly limited, constitutional monarchy. The kirk understood that royal power was not unlimited, that kings were responsible not just to God alone but in a very real sense to their subjects too, and that the relationship between God, prince and people formed a:

> band and contract to be mutual and reciprocal in all times coming between the prince and God and also between the prince and faithful people according to the Word of God.

Presbyterianism, in short, stood for representative and constitutional government in the church in a way in which episcopacy, linked as it was to royal control, could never purport to espouse.

91

*J*ames Graham, Marquis of Montrose, Covenanter and
Royalist. Painting by Honthorst.

In reacting against such an emphasis which seemed to diminish
his kingly powers, James VI advanced his own ideas on divine-right
monarchy and embarked on one of the major campaigns of his life. His
ambitious aim was to remodel the church's government and worship to
suit his tastes, first, by securing a foothold within the church for his
bishops and, then, by enhancing the bishops' powers and reducing the
authority of the general assembly. Nor was James over-scrupulous in the
means he adopted to achieve his ends. By a mixture of guile and force,
he succeeded in having his way. Yet the so-called compromise which
James achieved in reality was no compromise, for the presbyterian courts
were firmly muzzled under episcopal control; and the King's liturgical
innovations merely worked mischief for his hapless successor.

Well-meaning though he may have been, Charles I hit on policies
which were simply suicidal. James VI had recognised the inherent difficulties but Charles showed no apprehension of the dangers involved;
and in the face of the suspicions aroused, it was impossible for Charles
to have his way. Not only did he manage to forfeit the goodwill of the
nobles, which James had devoted a lifetime building up, but he also
succeeded in strengthening the presbyterian opposition which James had
outmanoeuvred. The nobles, on whom the King ultimately depended

for power, felt threatened by his Act of Revocation, which proposed to revoke all grants from crown and kirk lands since 1540. Charles, it is true, shifted his ground somewhat in the process, but the nobles no longer trusted him. They were also antagonised by Charles' method of government and exasperated by the political power which was accorded to the bishops.

At the same time, Charles set about moulding the Scottish church into the desired shape by reviving the liturgical changes which James VI had set aside on account of the opposition they had incurred. The King himself had used the English Prayer Book and Anglican ceremonial in worship during his visit to Edinburgh in 1633, which seemed a portent of changes to come, and he had insisted on his right to dictate the apparel of churchmen, including use of the surplice which the Scots had jettisoned at the Reformation as the 'badges of idolaters in the very act of their idolatry'. The introduction of a Book of Canons, inspired by Laud, caused much resentment, for it reaffirmed royal supremacy over the church and exalted still further the position and power of bishops but made no mention of what remained of the presbyterian system of courts. It also gave offence by the way in which it was imposed. It was forced on the church simply as an exercise of the King's prerogative. Then came the imposition of the Prayer Book of 1637 which, for the most part, was innocent in itself but was liable to be misconstrued, and it had as its model the English book. It also arrived at a bad time amid a growing atmosphere of fear and distrust. Organised rioting resulted, the conflict grew and the King's government in Scotland broke down. Charles had paid the price for alienating the sympathy of the nobles. The National Covenant in 1638 declared the church's doctrines and practices to be secured by numerous acts of parliament and concluded no innovations in the church could be legally made unless approved by 'free' general assemblies and parliaments. Though not so condemned in the Covenant, the bishops became the next target of the opposition. Thereafter, the ability of the general assembly and parliament to meet in unusual circumstances, free at any rate from royal manipulation, gave constitutional sanction to the work of the Covenanters behind whom much of Scotland had united.

The general assembly, the first to have met in twenty years, undid the work of the 'six pretended assemblies' which had met under royal pressure since 1606; it abolished episcopacy and condemned the infamous 'Five Articles' in worship, along with the Service Book, the Code of Canons, the Ordinal and the High Commission. Parliament, in turn, abolished the ecclesiastical estate in parliament, confirmed the assembly's actions and returned the church's legal status to the presbyterian constitution of 1592. Yet the fragile unity of the covenanting cause soon disintegrated, as dissensions emerged among moderates disillusioned with the course of events and with the increasingly militant tendencies at work within the movement. Bitter disagreement also arose over the wisdom of allying with the English parliamentarians in the Solemn League and Covenant of 1643 which led to civil war in Scotland and to the emergence of an effective royalist party.

The execution of Charles I rocked the new government of the theocrats or extreme Covenanters who had seized power in 1648 and who had attempted to render their opponents powerless by the curious Act of Classes in 1649. All Scots, however, united in accepting Charles II as King, but there agreement ended. The royalists were willing to accept Charles virtually without conditions attached, and the presbyterians found themselves seriously divided on the conditions they wished to impose. This was an ideal situation for Charles to exploit by speaking fair to all parties but committing himself to none. Indeed, while playing for time by negotiating with the Covenanters, Charles had commissioned Montrose to raise a royalist army to overthrow the government of the Covenanters but Montrose's capture and execution in 1650 forced Charles to make peace with his opponents in Scotland and to accept the Covenants which he so disliked. But Scottish acceptance of the King inevitably led to war with Cromwell and to an enforced union of the two countries. It was evident, however, that Scotland was run by an English administration and ruled by alien institutions, for after 1653 the Scottish parliament, privy council and general assembly were not allowed to meet.

In the end, Charles II was restored basically because the Protector-ate had failed to make itself popular in England where the King was restored, on terms, by his ex-enemies. But no fresh guarantees were forthcoming in Scotland where Charles had been accepted as King since 1650. After 1660, however, the church settlement proved notoriously difficult. Although the presbyterians represented a slight majority of the nation, the episcopalians were particularly strong north of the Tay and were much more influential at court. Yet the deceitful and underhand manner in which episcopacy was restored in 1662 caused great disgruntlement; and general uneasiness increased with the Act Rescissory which was aimed against the presbyterians and constitutionalists by sweeping away every piece of legislation since 1633. Nor were matters helped by the bad team whom Charles picked to govern the country.

One highly ill-advised measure, which the government would have been wise to let drop, was the act of 1662 designed to regularise the position of those ministers who had been appointed to benefices, since the act of 1649 abolishing patronage, by forcing them to accept presentation by a patron and episcopal collation. More than a quarter of the country's ministers declined to accept such a settlement and so were driven from their charges, thereby contributing to the highly dangerous problem of

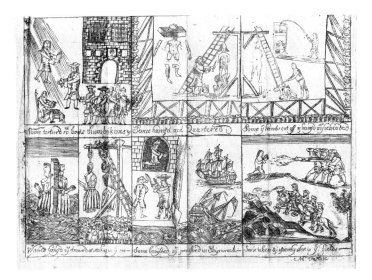

*The persecution of the Covenanters in the seventeenth century.
Frontispiece from Woodrow's* A Cloud of Witnesses, *1720.*

conventicles. The quartering of troops on the disaffected south-west resulted in the Pentland rising and, with its suppression, to a change of policy in favour of offering indulgences to peaceable 'outed' ministers. But the murder of Archbishop Sharp and the repressive policies pursued by the regime resulted in a further Westland rising, suppressed at Bothwell Brig.

Still the extreme Covenanters refused to come to terms with the government and so persecution was stepped up in the 1670s and 1680s, which led to sporadic guerilla warfare in the south-west. Most dissident presbyterians came to accept their lot, but a small minority of desperate presbyterians – the Cameronians – demanded a full implementation of the Covenants. Their manifestoes, issued in 1680 in the form of the Queensferry paper and Sanquhar declaration, consisted of a curious blend of religious fanaticism and constitutional ideas which swept aside divine-right monarchy in favour of a contractual monarchy, in which Charles II was declared to have forfeited the throne for renouncing the Covenants and James was declared ineligible as a Catholic.

With the assumption of power in Scotland by James, first as Duke of York and then as King, people increasingly became convinced of the government's despotism. Even stronger coercion of religious recalcitrants ensued, as government by inquisition reached new heights. Yet the failure of Argyll's rebellion in Scotland and Monmouth's in England suggests that public opinion had not sufficiently turned against James, who still had Scotland tightly in his grip. The established episcopal church, whose position depended on the crown's goodwill, dreaded opposing James' plans lest it, too, was dragooned into submission in the same sort of way as the regime had acted against the presbyterians. Indeed, James' initial success merely encouraged him to pursue policies which it would have been wiser to let lie. He advanced the interests of his loyal Catholic subjects at a reckless speed and in a manner which thoroughly alarmed his suspicious Protestant subjects.

When Revolution arrived, however, the initiative came from England. But even in Scotland James lost his nerve and let the government slip away from him, so enabling William's supporters to seize control. The Convention of estates, soon won over to the Williamite cause, proceeded to define the nature of the Revolution settlement. Constitutional issues, embodied in the Claim of Right and Articles of Grievances, focused on the need to obtain a legally-based monarchy. The existing constitution had come under fire and no mere change of monarch would suffice for those in the Convention who saw the Revolution as a wonderful opportunity to reform the constitution of state and church alike. For a start, the abolition of the committee of the articles freed parliament from the traditional shackles of royal manipulation. Though amenable to the gentle art of management, the legislature was at least potentially free to express its judgments. In the church, episcopal government was abolished in July 1689 but nothing immediately was put in its place. A sound Dutch Calvinist though he was, William preferred to retain bishops as pawns in the game, but he found them unco-operative and Jacobite in their sympathies. He was therefore forced to yield to parliament and to accept in 1690 the return of presbyterian church government, not on the covenanting model but on the comparatively mild model of the act of 1592. At the same time, the act of 1669 asserting royal supremacy over the church was rescinded; and lay patronage in the church was likewise removed.

The far-reaching changes effected, even if sometimes the product of compromise, were the outcome of tensions which had been building up over the preceding century. The Revolution enabled most southern Scots – and perhaps even a majority of Scots – to turn their backs with comparative ease on the last Stewart King, so ending an unbroken line of twelve Stewart sovereigns. It also ushered in an instability in politics which made the task of government more complex and less effective for both William himself and his successor, Queen Anne, the last Stewart ruler. In addition, the settlement created the conditions which made imperative a reassessment of the unsatisfactory nature of the regal link between the two countries. It was not for nothing that William in despair commended union as the solution to Scotland's troubles. But it was a solution which then found little support in Scotland and even less in England.

# CHAPTER VIII

# Covenanting, Revolution and Municipal Enterprise

## ALLAN I. MACINNES

The Scottish revolt against Charles I was instituted at the general assembly held in Glasgow between November 22nd and December 20th, 1638. The general assembly was attended by about 165 ministers and 100 elders (lay commissioners) from burghs and presbyteries. Its composition, proceedings and agenda were rigorously managed by the Tables, the disaffected element opposed to the continuance of Charles I's personal rule. The Tables had co-ordinated the petitioning against the authoritarian imposition of religious innovations in the months following the riots against the Service Book in Edinburgh in July 1637, petitioning which had culminated in their issuing of the National Covenant on February 28th, 1638. A nationalist as well as a deceptively radical manifesto, the National Covenant was intent on imposing fundamental limitations on monarchical power.

Conceded by Charles I in an effort to placate opposition to his personal rule, the general assembly not only effected the religious objectives of the National Covenant but perpetrated three acts of constitutional defiance which served as a British model for revolution. The assembly refused to dissolve when instructed by the King's commissioner, James Hamilton, Marquess of Hamilton. Continuing its proceedings the assembly abjured and removed episcopacy in favour of presbyterianism as the national polity for the kirk. At the conclusion of its proceedings, the assembly asserted its right to appoint the time and place of its next meeting, a right hitherto regarded as part of the royal prerogative. Over the next three years the Covenanting movement accomplished a political revolution which formally vested constitutional authority in parliament and reduced the role of monarchy to that of a cypher in Scotland. In practice, political power was to be vested in a radical oligarchy of nobles, gentry and burgesses, whose leadership of the Covenanting movement was supported by the ministers. Centralised demands for ideological conformity, financial supply and military recruitment were implemented in the localities by committees of radical activists. Within a British context, the constitutional defiance of the monarchy at Glasgow not only provoked the Bishops' Wars, but obliged Charles to summon first the 'short' then the 'long' parliaments in England in 1640. Instead of mobilising support against the Scottish

# THE
# PROTESTATION
## OF THE GENERALL
### *ASSEMBLIE OF THE*
#### CHVRCH OF SCOTLAND, AND OF
#### THE NOBLEMEN, BARONS,
##### *GENTLEMEN, BORROWES, MI-*
##### *NISTERS AND COMMONS;*

**Subſcribers of the Covenant, lately**
renewed, made in the high Kirk, and at the
*Mercate Croſſe* of Glaſgow, *the* 28, *and* 29.
*of November* 1638.

Printed at *Glaſgow* by *George Anderſon,*
*in the Yeare of Grace,* 1638.

*Not-so-obedient servants – title page of the 'Protestation'*
*against Charles I's religious policies issued by the*
*Covenanters' General Assembly in November 1638.*

Covenanters, the 'long' parliament especially became the national forum which co-ordinated dissent and paved the way for revolution in England.

Glasgow had been chosen as the venue for the assembly in the mistaken belief that the city's proximity to the Marquess of Hamilton's estates would facilitate intimidation by his kinsmen, tenantry and associates in Lanarkshire. This belief was mistaken on three counts. The Tables were able to mobilise superior forces in west-central Scotland. The marquess's estates were actually controlled by his mother, the indomitable Lady Anna Cunningham, a committed Presbyterian and Covenanting activist. Glasgow was pre-eminently a merchant city, the only town in the west of Scotland not beholden to nobles or gentry either for guidance in running its affairs or for clientage in promoting its interests nationally.

In terms of national standing, Glasgow was second only to Edinburgh as a commercial centre, but an aversion to taxation meant that the city was rarely higher than eighth in the formal rankings of royal burghs. Its mercantile community, and in particular the merchant adventurers trading with Scandinavia, the Baltic, France and the United Provinces, exercised the dominant influence over the town council. Nonetheless, Glasgow did not enjoy the liberty routinely accorded to royal burghs in its internal government.

Despite being an established trade centre nationally and internationally since the late twelfth century, Glasgow was not officially erected a royal burgh until 1611. But this erection, which reaffirmed the right of the Archbishop of Glasgow to nominate the provost and select the magistrates from a leet (short list) of potential bailies supplied by the town council, denied the city the freedom to elect its own magistrates. That the denial of this freedom remained a source of grievance was attested by the irregular submission of leets to archbishops. (Nine names were expected to be forwarded for the selection of three bailies.) The abolition of episcopacy at the general assembly of 1638 accorded the town council full control over the election of magistrates from 1639.

The merchants in their constitutional sparring with the archbishops were generally supported by the craft guilds. Since the early sixteenth century, fourteen crafts had been established as self-regulating and self-supporting corporations under their own deacons. In keeping with the provisions of the letter of guildry of 1605, designed to promote harmony between the merchant and craft guilds, the crafts elected annually a deacon convener for all the crafts who presided over the Trades House and sat on the town council *ex officio* as a magistrate, along with the dean of guild. Although the dean of guild, like the provost, was always a merchant, four of the eight members of his council charged to regulate the commercial affairs of the city were craftsmen. As well as securing one of the three posts as bailies, craftsmen normally filled twelve of the twenty-five places on the town council.

Such was the latitude afforded to the participation of craft guilds in municipal government, that Glasgow was twice reprimanded – in 1628 and 1636 – by the Convention of Royal Burghs, the national agency for the conservation of burgh privileges in general and mercantile dominance in particular. Indeed, it was not until 1637, following further strictures from the Convention, that the procedure for the election of the town council was regularised to ensure that the outgoing and incoming magistrates controlled its composition. The oligarchic and self-perpetuating nature of municipal government was not altered fundamentally by the emergence of the Covenanting movement which, in 1641, limited officeholding by magistrates to one year followed by a two-year gap before resuming office. Hitherto, magistrates in Glasgow had tended to serve no more than three years consecutively in office.

The control over municipal government exercised by the merchant and craft guilds should not eclipse the contribution of the professional classes to civic life. Notwithstanding the concentration of wealth and power in the hands of merchant adventurers, lawyers were profitably engaged in the working of money and the acquisition of land in and around the city. Indeed, the most momentous contribution to the welfare of the city in the reign of Charles I was provided by a legal family, the Hutchesons of Lambhill. The gift of George Hutcheson in December 1639 of £13,333.6s.8d. Scots (£1,111.2s.3d. Sterling – there were twelve Scots pounds to one pound sterling between 1603 and 1707), to establish a hospital for merchants, craftsmen and other traders who were 'now old decrepit men above 50 years of age', was complemented by a series of bequests by his brother Thomas in 1641. Thomas not only added land and a legacy of £7,000 Scots to the hospital but, with endowments of £20,133.6s.8d. Scots, instituted a school for indigent orphans from burgess families.

The regional importance of the city had been notably enhanced by the establishment of the Faculty of Physicians and Chirurgeons in 1599, a specialised complement to the intellectual contribution made by the University of Glasgow since 1451. Although the university was persistently in financial difficulties in the reign of Charles I, the town council launched the decade-long campaign to raise funding for a college library and the general refurbishment of buildings and grounds, with a donation of £1,333.6s.8d in 1630.

The town council was actively involved in an extensive programme of construction, a programme which was intent on improving both the material and the spiritual environment of the city. Accordingly, in the course of Charles I's personal rule, the town council invested heavily in deepening the Clyde, in repairing and maintaining the bridges across the river, erecting a new tollbooth, repairing and refurbishing kirks and taking over responsibility from the archbishop for paying stipends to city ministers. The holding of the general assembly in the cathedral (the high kirk under presbyterianism) afforded a show-piece for the town council to project the city's flourishing image, not only by sponsoring and supervising alterations to the cathedral's structure and interior, but by masterminding the allocation of lodgings for ministers, elders, legal assessors and the accompanying escort of the Tables; by continuing a watch for the duration of the assembly; by cleaning up the streets and removing the poor indoors where they were maintained by a stent (local levy). More pertinently for the developing political situation, the town council paid the expenses of George Anderson to remove from Edinburgh and establish his printing press in the city in readiness for the assembly. In the event, the first printing press in the city was not fully operational until 1640.

In recognition of its improvement programme, Glasgow's privileges as a royal burgh were confirmed in the parliament held to mark the Scottish coronation of Charles I in 1633 and again in 1636, when the city was obliged to pay a yearly duty of £13.6s.8d. Scots to the crown in addition to the £10.13.4d. Scots paid annually to the archbishop. This additional payment, though resented, was deemed imperative because of interminable wrangling with the other royal burghs on the Clyde over respective trading precincts. In substance, wrangling represented a clash of rival priorities, that of Glasgow to promote commercial enterprise against that of other burghs to conserve trading privileges. The volume of trade generated by Glasgow was six times that of the other leading towns in the west of Scotland. Because of the shallowness of the Clyde in its approach to the city, ships of twenty tons or over were obliged to load or unload cargoes within the trading precincts claimed by Dumbarton and Renfrew. While ships wholly owned by Glasgow merchants were exempt from loading dues, a considerable proportion of the city's continental trade – in excess of 80 per cent during the 1630s – was carried in charter vessels liable to petty customs and other such charges scaled to the size of the ship, the nature of its cargo and its duration at anchor. Freelance shipping drawn to the Clyde by the commercial pull of Glasgow was obliged to offer up half its cargoes to either or both other burghs. Before the resort to arbitration commanded by the Covenanting leadership in 1641, Glasgow's mercantile community vented their frustrations by instigating masters of chartered ships not to pay the exorbitant charges levied by Dumbarton and Renfrew.

Glasgow's dominance of commercial activity of the whole Firth of Clyde and the western seaboard was reflected in and stimulated by its growing population. With purportedly over 5,000 communicants within the city and another 1,000 in the adjacent barony parish, Glasgow had a population approaching five figures that was unmatched by any urban or rural parish in the west of Scotland. The population growth which

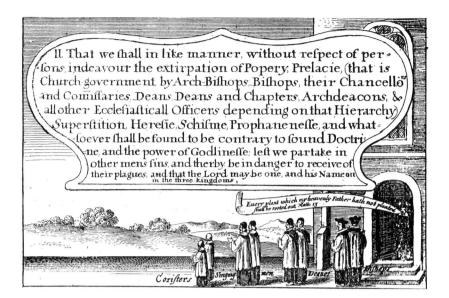

II. That we shall in like manner, without respect of persons, indeavour the extirpation of Popery, Prelacie, (that is Church-government by Arch-Bishops, Bishops, their Chancello and Comissaries, Deans, Deans and Chapters, Archdeacons, & all other Ecclesiasticall Officers depending on that Hierarchy) Superstition, Heresie, Schisme, Prophanenesse, and whatsoever shall be found to be contrary to sound Doctrine, and the power of Godlinesse; lest we partake in other mens sins, and therby be in danger to receive of their plagues, and that the Lord may be one, and his Name on in the three kingdoms,

*Euery plant which my heavenly Father hath not planted shall be rooted out. Matth. 15*

Coristers    Singing    men    Deacon

*W*encelaus Hollar's illustrated version of the 'Solemn League and Covenant'; its anti-episcopalian religious thrust also reflected economic self-interest among its Scottish lay adherents.

prompted the town council to acquire the estate of Gorbals immediately to the south of the river was, simultaneously, promoting the domestic demand for coal extracted from the city's hinterland – notably around the town of Partick to the west – as also the droving trade in black cattle from the Highlands and Islands.

The threat to commercial enterprise posed by Charles I's policy of economic uniformity throughout the British Isles was a significant factor in motivating not only Glasgow but landed society in the city's hinterland to support the Covenanting movement. Led by Glasgow, the commercial interest in the west of Scotland moved in concert to oppose the common fishing and tariff reform. With up to 600 boats from the Firth of Clyde regularly engaged in the pursuit of herring and white fish from June to January, the fishing industry was not only the principal source of employment for whole communities, but the major currency earner for the west of Scotland in overseas markets. The court's effort to vest exclusive rights to deep-sea and in-shore fishing throughout the British Isles – save for two reserved areas in the Firths of Forth and Clyde – in a society of adventurers was imperfectly effected in 1632, in the teeth of opposition from western landlords no less than burgesses.

The King's proposed increase in customs rates (from 5 to 7 per cent) on all exports and all goods temporarily offloaded in Scotland engaged the full ire of the region's commercial interest in 1636. As well as rendering all staple exports to the continent uncompetitive, the equalising of Scottish with English tariffs threatened to disrupt and dislocate three particular areas of expansion in the west – the overland pack-horse trade in yarn and coarse cloth, the droving trade to England and the carrying trade to Ulster. Rent rolls and trading ledgers in the west were being jeopardised by an absentee King who was being clearly identified as a danger to the prosperity of the city and the region. At the same time, religious innovations were being promulgated from the court with marked insensitivity to Scottish sensibilities.

Commercial factors certainly underscored opposition to religious innovations in and around Glasgow. In anticipation of ecclesiastical censure at the general assembly, a composite indictment against the life and doctrine of Patrick Lindsay as Archbishop of Glasgow was formulated at the behest of the Tables in October 1638. In addition to stereotyped pastoral deficiencies, Archbishop Lindsay was accused of manipulating fiars prices – the rates at which rents and duties paid in kind were commuted into money. Indeed, the feuars, the heritable tenants of the archbishop in and around Glasgow, had withheld their annual duties in 1635 in protest against the high rates of fiars prices exacted by the archbishop – from 11 to 27 per cent higher than fiars exacted by the crown and other landlords in the west of Scotland.

Arrears in duties, totalling £4,633.9s.4d. Scots, left the archbishop in straitened circumstances and personally compromised as public disturbances marked the reception of the Service Book in the summer of 1637: a situation exploited by opportunist ministers, notably John Bell the elder, a venerated presbyterian who was to commence proceedings at the general assembly, and Zachary Boyd, a prolific author of devotional tracts. They exacted a bond from the archbishop in August 1637 which not only gave them priority in the payment of stipends over other ministers in and around the city. But, in return for advancing £992 Scots at 4 per cent (half the current rate of interest), they secured an effective veto over the disposal of the teinds (tithes) and rents of the archbishopric.

Glasgow affords the prime illustration of the importance of political over religious considerations in determining support for the Covenanting movement in the west of Scotland. The presbytery of Glasgow, covering the city and its immediate hinterland, was the first of the western presbyteries to react against Archbishop Lindsay's directive for the purchase of two copies of the Service Book for every parish by August 1637. Nonetheless, only a committed minority of ministers were prepared to petition the privy council for the suspension of this directive. The city did stage a day-long riot against religious innovations on Thursday August 30th, which matched the protests against the Service Book in Edinburgh on July 23rd, both with respect to its tumultuous intensity and the involvement of women of substance as instigators of public disturbances. As in Edinburgh, the magistrates made no effort to investigate the rioting. Unlike the rioting in the capital, however, the disturbances in Glasgow were not directed against readings from the Service Book, but against the reported sermon in favour of a new liturgy delivered by William Annand, minister of Ayr, to the diocesan synod meeting in the city the previous day: a time lapse which fuels suspicion that the harrying of Annand from the city was stage-managed.

The town and presbytery were jointly identified with the mass movement of supplicants which evolved into the Tables. Yet even though the National Covenant generally received a favourable reception, considerable reservations were expressed by merchants and physicians as by ministers and academics about its radical interpretation by the Covenanting leadership. So widespread were these reservations not only within the city but among landowners in the presbytery, that the Covenanting leadership despatched a special delegation to Glasgow at the end of July 1638. The continuing reservations of an influential sector within the city and presbytery led to a notably favourable reception for the proclamation of the King's Covenant, a conservative alternative to the National Covenant, on September 24th.

The hopes of Hamilton that the location of the general assembly in Glasgow would not inevitably lead to the abolition of episcopacy and the establishment of presbyterianism were diminished, but not dashed, when a further delegation from the Covenanting leadership was required to secure the return of Hugh Montgomery, Earl of Eglinton, as elder for the presbytery of Glasgow. When the general assembly commenced on November 21st, Patrick Bell, the Provost of Glasgow, was not so much the representative but the delegate of the town council, which he was obliged to consult before casting his vote on any issue of substance. In the event, the town council supported the assembly's acts of constitutional defiance. Moreover, the commitment of the commercial interest to the political ends of the Covenanting movement was wholehearted and effected virtually without demur over the next three years, ideologically, financially and militarily.

Military preparations were actually under way in the city during the summer of 1638. By the advent of the general assembly not only was Glasgow being policed by a watch, but sixty young men had been trained in the handling of arms by a drill-master brought from Edinburgh. In the months prior to the outbreak of the Bishops' Wars, the purchase of arms and ammunition was stepped up, markedly from February 1639 when a stent, or local tax, was instituted for this purpose. In April, 100 men had been despatched to join the Covenanting vanguard watching the Borders and the first city company had been raised, equipped and trained in advance of the directive from Edinburgh for a general muster.

*A*lexander Henderson (left) *and John Bell* (right), *leading presbyterian ministers in the campaign against the Prayer Book, which culminated in the initiative of the Covenant.*

A further eight companies were undergoing regular training on Glasgow Green by the end of May, when the city was divided into quarters to expedite military recruitment – one year in advance of its quartering to enhance ecclesiastical discipline and religious observance. Apart from the vanguard and recrews or reinforcements, only the first company was actually mobilised in the course of the First Bishops' War, the remainder being held in reserve to guard against loyalist invasion on the western seaboard.

When mobilisation resumed for the Second Bishops' War, two companies generously provided with 144 men each and supplemented by occasional recrews of fifty were despatched to the Borders during July and were subsequently engaged on active service in the north of England. In addition to military expenditure incurred from the advent of mobilisation in summer 1640 until the last return of troops from England in autumn 1641, the craft guilds had continued to provide tents, shoes, stockings and perishable provisions 'at the common charge'. Gold and silver plate to value of £1,500 Scots was sent to Edinburgh on the security of the town council. Six leading citizens, headed by Thomas Hutcheson of Lambhill voluntarily donated £5,666.13s.4d. Scots. Moreover, Glasgow's portion of the national debts to the factors at Campvere for the purchase of arms and ammunition in the United Provinces – assigned at £8,900.10s. Scots in May 1641 – was raised within four months by 168 burgesses voluntarily stenting themselves up to £333.6s.8d. each.

In total, the city of Glasgow directly expended £19,529.7s.8d. Scots in support of the Covenanting movement in the course of the Bishops' Wars. The city, like the other leading Scottish towns, had to bear the hidden cost of stops to trade during 1639 and 1640. Glasgow actively supported the sinking of two ships in the Clyde to deny the royalists passage to Dumbarton Castle during the Bishops' War. Moreover, the city readily agreed to service the transportation of 5,000 troops to suppress rebellion in Ireland after the commissioning of a Covenanting expeditionary force in December 1641.

Over the next decade, the city tended to back the radical mainstream's political direction of the Covenanting movement. As well as supplying Covenanting forces in Ireland: the city supported armed intervention on the side of the parliamentarians in the first English Civil War from 1644. However, the magistrates and town council were compromised politically by negotiating with the royalist leader, James Graham, Marquess of Montrose, after his final victory at nearby Kilsyth in August 1645. The city was fined £40,000 Scots by the Covenanting leadership. The magistrates and town council were dismissed from office after a short spell of imprisonment in Edinburgh; an action which provoked a mass demonstration in the city instigated by displaced councillors, who were temporarily restored in June 1648, after their successors were in turn incarcerated and dismissed for opposing the Engagement.

This diplomatic alliance of conservative Covenanters with Charles I to secure Scottish intervention in the Second English Civil War ended in failure that August. The restoration of a radical regime nationally was complemented by the restoration of the radical faction in city government by October.

Purging from office coincided with the scourging of the city by plague from November 1646. The plague, which was carried from England by the Covenanting troops brought back to crush royalist resistance, was still virulent when the radicals resumed power. There were to be no further purgings from municipal office despite a split in the radical ranks nationally over support for Charles II, following the execution of his father in England in January 1649. The radical majority in Glasgow pragmatically supported the patriotic accommodation with the royalists to fend off Cromwellian occupation. When this ominous prospect became a reality in 1651, city pragmatism found remunerative expression through commercial enterprise. The opening up of the English colonial trade during the 1650s laid the foundations of the city's prosperity over the next 150 years – albeit Glasgow was to flourish illicitly between the Restoration of 1660 and the Treaty of Union of 1707 by disregarding the reimposition of the English Navigation Laws.

# CHAPTER IX

# The Century of the Three Kingdoms

DAVID STEVENSON

For the British Isles the seventeenth century was very much 'the Century of the Three Kingdoms'. On the one hand the three kingdoms were, for the first time, ruled by a single monarch. On the other, the century saw intermittent attempts by the lesser kingdoms, Scotland and Ireland, to escape English domination by adjusting their relationships with their great neighbour in their favour. These attempts failed – and indeed had the opposite effects to those intended. By the early years of the eighteenth century England had triumphed, the lesser kingdoms had been subdued.

The three kingdom state came into existence through the dynastic accident of James VI of Scotland ascending the English throne as James I in 1603; and in the same year the centuries-old English claim to rule all Ireland came much closer to reality than ever in the past, through the completion of the Elizabethan conquest by the submission of the native Irish of Ulster. The relationships of the lesser kingdoms to the greater was thus very different. Ireland was not only constitutionally subordinate to the English crown, she was also newly conquered territory. Scotland, by contrast, was at least nominally an equal partner with England in a union which might be accidental but which was widely regarded as a happy dispensation. The Scots believed that their interests and those of the English were fully compatible; far from seeing their country's position as paralleling that of Ireland as a lesser kingdom in the new state, the Scots sympathised with (and were willing to help in) English plans to complete the subjection of Ireland. England's 'Irish problem' was indeed seen as in some ways similar to Scotland's 'Highland problem'. In each case the political autonomy and the cultural and linguistic identity of Gaelic peoples were under attack.

Not only had the Irish and Highland problems similarities, they were linked through the close ties between the peoples of the West Highlands and the Gaelic Irish. In the past, Highland rebels had frequently found safe refuge among their kinsmen in Ireland, and large numbers of Highland clansmen had fought in Irish wars. The union of the crowns now enabled action against the Gaels to be co-ordinated. Military help from Ireland was used to help subdue West Highland rebels; and the Scots enthusiastically joined the English in the Jacobean plantation of Ulster, a massive colonisation scheme aimed at destroying the Gaelic society of the province once and for all.

Such co-operation helped reassure the Scots that they and the English formed a dominant partnership in the three kingdoms, with Ireland in the dependent, subject role. Scots belief that this was the position was strengthened by the fact that they had supplied the dynasty which now ruled the three kingdoms. Yet from the first the Scots needed such reassurance, for they must have had at the back of their minds a fear that the union could develop very differently. England had five times the population of Scotland, and the disparity in wealth was even greater. So far as the English were concerned the union of the crowns was certainly welcome. It provided an undisputed Protestant succession, and ended the possibility of Scotland being used (as often in the past) as France's back door into England. But in English eyes there was no question of equal partnership with Scotland. Traditionally the Scots were despised as backward and poverty-stricken, and in the years before 1603 Scotland had been, in English eyes, virtually a client state whose king was dependent on an English pension. The mere fact that her king was now also king of England could not suddenly elevate Scotland to equality. Whatever the theoretical relationship of the two kingdoms, the English assumed that Scotland would become a subordinate kingdom like Ireland.

James saw the potential dangers of such varying Scottish and English interpretations of unions, and therefore proposed a complete union, a merging of the two kingdoms into the single kingdom of Great Britain, as a solution. But he soon had to abandon such plans. The English were hostile, seeing no advantage to themselves and fearing some plot by their Scottish King to give his countrymen undue influence in English affairs; and the Scots were understandably suspicious of the likely long term consequences for their national identity of merging with so much larger a partner. The failure of James' plans meant that England and Scotland remained linked only through his person as king, but it soon became clear that if he could not have formal closer union he intended to make the two kingdoms as like each other as possible; and the adjustments necessary to achieve this were to be one-sided, involving the anglicisation of Scotland. Similarly, in such all-British matters as foreign affairs and economic policy, English interests were to have priority. Given England's preponderance this was almost inevitable, but this did not make it any more palatable to the Scots. That Scotland's future was to lie in anglicisation and subordination to an anglicised crown, made much more powerful than in the past by union, became far more obvious once Charles I succeeded his father in 1625. Charles might be Scots by birth and blood, but in upbringing, manners and sympathies he was wholly English. Scotland's native dynasty had been captured and anglicised by an alien English court.

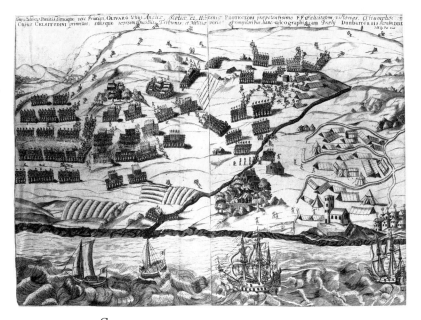

*Scottish attempts to reform the union in their favour in the 1640s eventually provoked English invasion; and, following Cromwell's great victory at Dunbar in 1650, victory.*

The effects of the union of the crowns thus threatened Scotland's identity and status. Discontent at Charles' innovations in religion was increased by the fact that they were changes aimed at achieving conformity with England. His attack on the power of the landowning classes was also perceived as linked to the union; it was his position as an absentee monarch with the power and prestige of the great English crown behind him that enabled him to attack such powerful vested interests.

The result was revolt in Scotland in 1637; and once this challenge emerged the imposing façade of Charles' power and success began to collapse in all three kingdoms. The covenanters set up their own provisional government and raised armies, and the bungling inadequacy of Charles' response destroyed the credibility of his regime. English opponents of royal policies were encouraged by Scotland's successful defiance, and (urged on by covenanting propaganda stressing that the English had grievances similar to those of the Scots) growing discontent prevented Charles from mobilising England's resources effectively to deal with the Scots. It is a measure of Charles' ineptitude that so many of his English subjects actually sympathised with their usually despised northern neighbours at this point!

The Covenanters soon concluded that direct interference in English affairs was necessary to protect their religious and constitutional

'*The Humble Petition of Jock of Braid*'. *The title page of a
tract of 1648. The petition complains of the civil war and
disturbances in Scotland and pleads for a better religious settlement.*

revolution. Since their King ruled more than one kingdom, they could
never achieve security by destroying royal power in Scotland alone. If
Charles reasserted his power successfully in England, it was obvious
he would then use English resources to overthrow the Covenanters.
Therefore when the Covenanters occupied the north of England in
1640 and forced him to ratify their revolution they also insisted that
he summon the English parliament and make it a party to the peace
settlement. Thus it was the Scots who brought the Long Parliament
into being, deliberately providing the King's English opponents with a
national forum in which to express themselves, an institution through
which to organise their attack on royal power.

Charles I now found his authority defied in both Scotland and
England. Inevitably he concluded that priority must be given to restoring
his position in England. Danger in the metropolitan kingdom had to take
priority over danger in a provincial one, even though it had been revolt in
the latter that began the crisis. The King therefore hastened to buy off the
Covenanters by (for the moment) surrendering royal power in Scotland
so he could concentrate on England.

However, developments in the third of the three kingdoms now
intervened. The Covenanters' revolt had had a destabilising effect in
Ireland as well as in England, and the situation there was complicated
by the presence of the Scots colonists in Ulster. Even before the Scots

revolt began the crown had come to regret having encouraged Scots participation in the plantation, and a campaign to stamp out religious dissidence among the Ulster Scots had been launched. Ireland was given a role in Charles' subsequent plans for invading Scotland, and there was discussion of driving out the Scots colonists to prevent them forming a fifth column in Ulster.

These schemes came to nothing, but, fatally, they involved arming and training thousands of Irish Catholics, either to invade Scotland or counter a feared Scots invasion of Ireland to protect the Scots colony. Arming Irish Catholics was directly contrary, for obvious reasons, to normal policy; and talk of destroying the Scots colony in Ulster gave hope of revenge to the Irish who had suffered loss of lands through the Ulster plantation. More widely, successful Scots defiance of royal power had roused intense excitement among those of the native Irish who were not reconciled to conquest. The Scots had revealed the fragility of royal and English power, and many of the Irish resolved to follow their example. Yet if the Irish revolt was partly inspired by the example of the Scots, it was also inspired by fear of them. The virulent anti-Catholic propaganda of the Covenanters and their boasts that they would destroy Catholicism throughout the British Isles raised fears that once they had defeated Charles I they would turn their attention to Irish Catholics.

The Scots revolt of 1637 thus contributed in several ways to the outbreak of the great Irish rising of 1641. The Irish rising in turn contributed directly to converting the constitutional crisis in England (itself induced by the Scots revolt) into civil war. The point at issue in the final break between the King and the English parliament was who should control forces to be raised to subdue the Irish, each side fearing that such forces might be employed in England against the other before proceeding to Ireland. As England collapsed into civil war, Scotland contributed again to the intricate war dance of the three kingdoms by sending a large army to Ulster to protect Protestants, and particularly Scots colonists, there against the Irish. Since Ireland was an English dependency the army was sent through a treaty with the English parliament, but the Scots also claimed a right to intervene in Ireland even without English approval, on two grounds: there was a 'Scottish colony' there, and Ulster in Irish Catholic hands would present a strategic threat to Scotland, being particularly likely to destabilise the West Highlands by encouraging Catholic Gaels there who were already hostile to the covenanters.

By 1642 a revolt which had begun with a riot in an Edinburgh church had widened into the War of the Three Kingdoms, in which the fate of each kingdom was closely linked with developments in the other two. In the years that followed the complexity of these interrelationships continued to increase.

Had the Scots not sent an army to Ulster, the Irish confederates might well have succeeded in overrunning all Ireland. The confederates soon identified the Scots as more formidable opponents than the weak Dublin government representing the King, and therefore in 1643 they made a truce or cessation with the King so they could concentrate their resources against the Scots. The King was willing to accept the cessation for similar reasons; he identified his most immediately dangerous enemy as the English parliament, and therefore wished to be free of the Irish war so he could concentrate on that in England. Victory was now in sight in England, with a series of royal successes demonstrating that Charles was gaining the upper hand over parliament. But again the 'three kingdoms' element intervened to prevent a quick decision.

The Scots decided that they could not afford to stand by and let the King triumph, for once he had crushed resistance in England he would surely turn to destroying the Covenanters' revolution as well. Therefore, in 1644 the Covenanters followed up their intervention in Ireland by sending an army into England. This tipped the military balance in parliament's favour; but it also provoked royalist revolt in Scotland led by the Marquess of Montrose. Scots intervention in England also led to the truce between the King and the Irish developing into an alliance, though one confined to the Scottish theatre of war. The Irish agreed to send an expeditionary force to Scotland to serve under the royalist Marquess of Montrose, hoping that this would undermine the Covenanters' hold on Scotland and force them to withdraw their army from Ireland.

The Irish force, reinforced by Catholic Highlanders, formed the nucleus of the army that Montrose led in his remarkable 'Year of Victories' in 1644–45; they were as much victories for Catholic Gaels as for the royalist cause. But ultimately Montrose's campaigns were a failure in the eyes of those who had sponsored them. He and the King had aimed at forcing the Covenanters to withdraw from the English Civil War, setting up a royalist regime in Scotland, and leading a new army into England to fight for Charles. The Irish had intended to force the Scots to withdraw from Ireland. But in the event the Covenanters managed to retain their armies in both kingdoms, though their sizes were reduced.

The main effect of Montrose's victories was that they greatly reduced the part played by the Scots in the English Civil War. They had counted on playing a decisive and dominant role in parliament's victory over the King and then being able to dominate a British peace settlement, which would remodel the union of the crowns on federal lines which would guarantee Scotland and England an equal say in British affairs, and establish permanent links between their two parliaments to prevent the King attempting in future to use the resources of one kingdom against the other. The English parliament, desperate for military help in 1643, had agreed to make such changes when peace was eventually restored, but the Scots' terms could never really be acceptable to the English: what was 'equal' about a federal union if it gave one million Scots equal weight to five million Englishmen? Moreover the Covenanters, made arrogant by earlier successes, were stupidly tactless about the way in which they intended to dictate a peace settlement primarily designed to protect Scotland's interests. Not surprisingly the result of all this was a strong anti-Scots backlash in the English parliament. This was intensified by the fact that the Scottish army in England, weakened by the need to send troops to oppose Montrose in Scotland, failed to take the leading part in defeating the King in England that had been expected. By the time Montrose was defeated and the Scots could again concentrate their attention on England, it was too late; the King had been defeated, but it was parliament's English armies that got the credit; and it was made clear that the Scots would not be allowed to alter the union in their interests in return for their help. The Scottish tail was not to wag the English dog.

The English parliament had emerged as the dominant force within Britain – and therefore as the main threat to other interests in all three kingdoms. Factions among both the confederate Irish and the Scottish Covenanters now began to argue that the best way to cope with the new situation would be to ally themselves with the defeated King, for now Charles had been totally defeated in England surely he would agree, in return for their help in retaining his metropolitan English throne, to whatever terms for an ultimate peace settlement they asked. In accordance with this logic moderate Covenanters agreed by the Engagement Treaty of 1647 to help the King regain power in England in return for him promising to adjust the union in Scotland's favour. In the eyes of the English parliament the Scots had changed sides; in their own eyes they were acting consistently to achieve the same end, protection for Scotland's interests. But the Engager's invasion of England in 1648 was totally defeated; and, in retaliation for the Second Civil War in England provoked by the Engagement, the English parliament executed Charles I and abolished the monarchy.

Thus the English answer to Scots demands for a new type of union was to destroy the only union that existed; that of the crowns. The Scots, however, were not ready to accept this. Charles might have been an Englishman in essentials, but he was a Scot by blood, and in executing the King of England the English had executed the King of Scots as well.

The young Charles II now had the choice of accepting help in regaining his English throne proffered by Irish Catholics or by Scots presbyterians. Ironically the lesser kingdoms which had begun the revolt against the crown now sought to restore it. Before Charles could make up his mind which offer to accept, Cromwell's astonishingly successful 1649 campaigns crushed Irish resistance, thus forcing the King into the hands of the Scots. This, in turn, provoked the Cromwellian conquest of Scotland in 1650–51. The War of the Three Kingdoms was over. The lesser kingdoms, which had revolted against the roles they were assigned within the three kingdom state under Charles I, now experienced a dramatic reassertion of English supremacy under Cromwell.

Neither Scotland nor Ireland could do anything but acquiesce in the unitary British state established by Cromwell, though this meant the abolition of their parliaments in return for token representation at Westminster. The reply to the Scottish demands for 'equal' federal union was thus the imposition of what England saw as 'equal' incorporating union, in which England predominated by right of weight of numbers as well as by conquest. When the Restoration of monarchy came in 1660, the lesser kingdoms, whatever their sympathies, took no active part either for or against; the memory of conquest was too recent for them to do anything but passively follow England's lead. In the final major political upheaval of the century however, the overthrow of James VII and II in 1688–89, the roles of the lesser kingdoms diverged. Scotland again accepted England's lead; opposition to the Catholic King had been growing, but after the disastrous results of Scotland trying to take the initiative in British affairs under the Covenanters action had to await events south of the border. But a Highland Jacobite rising indicated that some Gaels at least saw virtues in the dethroned James, and their Catholic Irish kinsmen gave him strong support. As in the 1640s, all Ireland would probably have fallen into Irish Catholic hands were it not for the presence of the Scots colonists in Ulster, though this time no army came from Scotland to support them. It took major campaigns in 1690–91 to crush James' attempts to use Ireland as a stepping-stone back to his British thrones.

With Scotland showing herself ready to follow England and the Catholic Irish so crushed that they were not to rise again for a century, England's domination of the three kingdoms seemed secure; but in fact there was a final challenge to face. The English parliament had gained greatly in prestige and pretensions to real power through legitimising the revolution against the 'tyrant' James and then virtually electing William and Mary as joint monarchs. But the Scottish parliament saw itself as having acted out a similar role, and expected an enhanced position in the state. Even the Irish parliament, in the hands of the Protestant minority, tried to benefit from the constitutional revolution by asserting itself against its English big brother. Moreover, in both Scotland and Ireland the fact that the English parliament now shared power with the King gave rise to new grievances.

Being governed by kings in England's interests had been bad enough, but at least these kings were recognised as legitimately exercising authority (as king of Scots and king of Ireland) in the lesser kingdoms. Increasingly in the last decade of the century it was not the king in person but king and English parliament which were influencing policies in the lesser kingdoms. In Ireland there was traditional constitutional justification for this, and the Irish parliament was comparatively easily dealt with by asserting Ireland's subordination to the 'imperial crown' and 'imperial parliament' of England; and the Irish Protestant constitutionalists' position was in any case weak, as it was clear to all that it was only England's power (and therefore England's favour) that maintained Protestant supremacy over the Catholic majority.

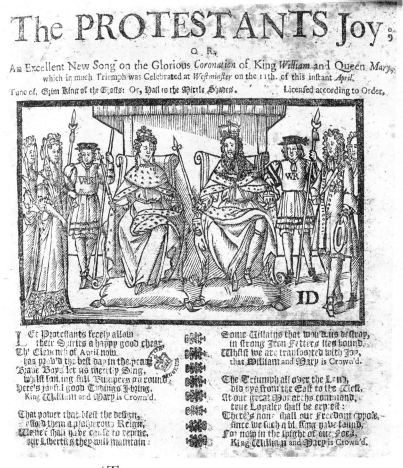

'The Protestant's Joy', a ballad in celebration of the
coronation of William and Mary, April 21st, 1689.

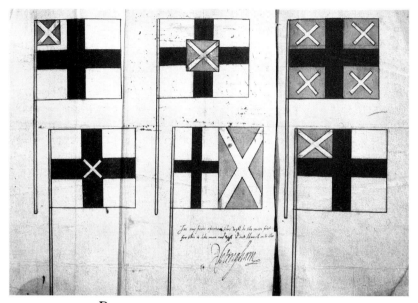

*Proposals for a union flag for Great Britain circa 1604.
Attempts to find a way of combining those of St George,
St Andrew and St Patrick in a way acceptable to the three
kingdoms led eventually to the Union Jack.*

The Scottish challenge was not so easy to deal with; English propagandist attempts to extend the 'imperial crown' argument to Scotland and thus claim that her parliament was subordinate to Westminster were indignantly met by assertions of the imperial status of the Scottish crown. The Scottish parliament's demands for a share in government placed King William in an impossible position, for he could sometimes only please one parliament by offending the other; as it was the English parliament he naturally tended to appease, Scottish feelings of grievance grew. When kings had held undisputed power, union of the crowns might prove workable, if awkward, with care. However, now parliaments claimed to share power, the monarch found incompatible policies pressed on him by parliaments representing the rival interests of two kingdoms. Not surprisingly William concluded that the solution lay in a union of parliaments.

In some respects the background to the union of parliaments recalls the efforts of the Covenanters to change the terms of the union in the 1640s. In both cases the English parliament was not, at first, interested, seeing no pressing reason for change, and in both cases the English only became interested when the Scots made such a nuisance of themselves that the English were forced to reconsider their relations with Scotland. Finally, in both instances the Scots ended up being forced to accept a union on English terms, very different from what they had originally wanted. In the 1640s the Scots had made the relations of the kingdoms a major issue in English politics through repeated military interventions in England. In the opening years of the eighteenth century they achieved the same results through acts of parliament.

The question of the succession to the crown provided an issue which epitomised the way in which the English parliament assumed it had authority in Scotland and, simultaneously, it provided the Scots with an opportunity to threaten English interests. In 1701 the English parliament legislated in favour of the Hanoverian succession. With remarkable insensitivity no attempt was made to consult Scotland, it evidently being taken for granted that, being virtually a subject state, she would hasten to do the same. Instead the Scots furiously rejected the Hanoverian succession, and threatened to break the union of the crowns on the death of Queen Anne and revert to independence, unless the union was adjusted so as to guarantee Scotland's autonomy. Other anti-English acts indicated Scotland's lack of commitment to the War of the Spanish Succession, as many Scots saw it as a war fought in England's interests into which Scotland had been dragged illegally.

These acts did indeed force the English to take seriously Scotland's grievances over the way in which the union was working. But their response demonstrated that if it came to threats England could do more damage to Scotland than Scotland to England. Unless Scotland agreed to negotiate a new union satisfactory to England, trade sanctions would be introduced which would bring disaster to Scotland's economy, already staggering under its most severe crisis for generations. The Scots decided to negotiate, but found their proposal for federal union swept aside by the English; they would only accept an incorporating union which would abolish the troublesome Scottish parliament.

The carrot and the stick were both employed to bring the Scots to agree. Major concessions to the Scots – including free trade and guarantees for her presbyterian established church and her legal system – were offered. But it was also made clear that if the Scots rejected these terms not only trade sanctions but war might follow. Memories of the humiliating Cromwellian conquest were still strong; incorporating union following one-sided negotiations would at least be better than incorporation following conquest. Further, Scots threats to break the union of the crowns were, in part at least, a bluff that had now been called. Few Scots were really ready to contemplate a return to independence; and where was an acceptable dynasty to be found if the Hanoverian line was rejected? The only alternative seemed to be to revert to the Stuarts, and substantial numbers of Jacobites would have favoured that. But to most Scots politicians submission to English terms for a new union and acceptance of the Protestant Hanoverian succession were preferable to opting for a Catholic dynasty and war with England. Thus in 1707 the Act of Union was passed as the lesser of evils and the Scottish parliament vanished.

The century of the three kingdoms, each trying to define its position within a single monarchy, was over. The English domination over the lesser kingdoms (which was to last into the twentieth century before being broken by Irish independence) was firmly established. There were still to be a few hiccoughs. The Scottish Jacobite risings of 1715 and 1745 were partly inspired by lingering opposition to the union of parliaments. Later in the century the Irish parliament sought, successfully at first, to assert its autonomy. But the revolt of the United Irishmen in 1798 starkly revealed the fragility of the Protestant ascendancy's hold over the Irish Catholic population, its ultimate complete dependence on the might of England, and the price exacted for continuing English support was abolition of the Irish parliament (and the nominally separate kingdom of Ireland) in 1801. The process of reducing three kingdoms and three parliaments into one, in the interests of the greatest of the three, was complete.

# CHAPTER X

# A Union Broken?
# Restoration Politics in Scotland

JOHN PATRICK

When Charles II was restored to the throne in 1660 he found England and Scotland united into one commonwealth. This union had been in *de facto* existence for nearly nine years, and there is a good deal of evidence to suggest that many Scots welcomed the firm and generally fair administration which resulted from it. Nonetheless, it was taken for granted at the Restoration that Charles would reinstate a separate Scottish administration. There were, indeed, compelling reasons for such a step. First, the union was essentially a republican institution, and was therefore bound to be suspect to the restored monarchy. Next, it was very unpopular in England, largely because it cost the English taxpayer a formidable sum every year to maintain. Finally, whatever 'the meaner sort' of Scot thought of it, Scottish nobles, clergy and lawyers all found their rights and privileges diminished by the union and were eager to be rid of it.

Accordingly, once the monarchy had been restored, the union was broken, and Scotland's national institutions were re-established in much the same form as before the Civil War. The Scottish privy council was reconstituted, and the Scottish parliament was once again summoned to sit in Edinburgh. To represent the King, a commissioner was appointed. He presided over parliament and signified the royal assent to the acts which it passed by touching them with his sceptre. At the Restoration this post, generally regarded as the head of the Scottish administration, went to John, Earl of Middleton, a brave and distinguished soldier. Like many Scots of his age and eminence he had at first fought for the Covenanting forces against the King in the Civil War. Since 1650 he had, however, been a prominent supporter of Charles II. Though an able soldier, as a politician he had serious defects. A direct and straightforward man, he favoured simple solutions for complex problems and had little time for subtlety or finesse. He was easily taken in, and tended to rely uncritically on the advice of his friends. At the time his 'heroic aspect' and 'manly eloquence', coupled with ten years' loyal service, overshadowed his defects, and his appointment as commissioner was widely welcomed. With a couple of exceptions the other Scottish ministers were cast in a similar mould, remarkable more for their loyalty than for political skill and experience.

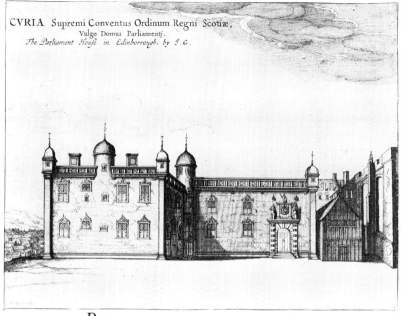

*Parliament House, Edinburgh, which was built in 1639.*

The commissioner's powers and those of the other Scottish officers of state were in fact very limited. The King was the real ruler of Scotland. Though Charles II was often casual and easy-going in personal matters, he took the powers and privileges of the monarchy very seriously indeed. He had a clear idea of his rights as King of Scotland, and had no intention of devolving any of them north of the border. So long as he was King, all important decisions on Scottish affairs had to be made in London. Charles' determination not to let the Scots off the leash was shared, for rather different reasons, by the Earl of Clarendon, his chief minister for the first seven years after the Restoration. Clarendon could never forget that the Civil War had begun in Scotland. He was deeply suspicious of all Scots, and wanted to keep Scotland under firm English control. Indeed, he probably regretted the decision to end the union. But both monarch and minister agreed that any institutions set up north of the border were to be merely executive and advisory. The heart of Scotland's government was to remain in London.

This was bound to lead to difficulties, largely because of Scotland's remoteness. It took at least five days for a despatch to travel between the two capitals, and politicians stationed in Edinburgh felt isolated and exposed. Part of their job was to send reports and advice to court, and they were clearly anxious to send the kind of advice and information which would be welcome at Whitehall. Once they had been in Scotland a month or two, however, they were out of touch with the court and had little chance of taking the political temperature in London. They therefore lived in constant fear of unwittingly causing offence by the reports and advice they submitted.

On the other hand, the administration in Scotland was expected to deal with certain matters on its own initiative. Some business was clearly too urgent or too minor to be referred to London. But it was difficult to know where to draw the line. Charles would not want to be pestered about trivia, but he would deeply resent not being consulted on matters of importance. Unfortunately what seemed important in Edinburgh might appear trivial in London – and vice versa. The difficulties were not all on one side. Whitehall was just as remote from Edinburgh as Edinburgh was from Whitehall, and Charles had not been to Scotland since 1651. He therefore had no up-to-date personal experience of the country and was forced to base his decisions largely on the advice and information sent down by his Scottish ministers, modified only by the views of his Whitehall staff. Thus the effective working of Scotland's government was hampered both by Edinburgh's ignorance of what was going on in London, and London's uncertainty about what was happening in Scotland.

In this situation an enormous amount depended on the secretary, who was the administration's link man in London. He handled all the correspondence between the King and his ministers in Scotland. Since all government business passed through his hands he could play an invaluable role. He could help the administration by filtering out material unworthy of Charles' attention, and by acting as the ministers' advocate, setting their actions in the best possible light. He could also keep Edinburgh in touch with developments in London and advise them what line to take where current problems were concerned. He might, on the other hand, adopt a critical stance, giving the King information which his other ministers were trying to suppress, or arguing against policies which they were advocating. For the ministers in Edinburgh, therefore, it was important that there should be a high level of mutual confidence between the secretary and the Edinburgh administration. In 1660 Clarendon's nominee for the post was the Earl of Newburgh who in many respects represented his ideal Scottish politician, since he had been educated in France, had married an English heiress, and had spent most of his life in the service of the King of Spain. The only Scottish things about him were his title and his estates. He had, however, little administrative experience and was passed over in favour of his rival for the post, the Earl of Lauderdale.

Lauderdale had played a leading part in Covenanting politics, and had seemed a convinced and enthusiastic presbyterian. An uncouth figure, liable to sudden outbursts of rage, he was also learned and intelligent, and proved adaptable enough to seem quite at home in environments as dissimilar as an assembly of divines and the court of Charles II. After the Restoration he made ribald jests about the Covenant, 'called himself and his nation a thousand rebels and traitors', and heaped eulogies on Clarendon and Middleton. It was an extraordinary performance, and it made many, including Clarendon and Middleton, believe that Lauderdale could not be trusted. In fact by 1660 he was first and foremost a professional politician who did not greatly care what beliefs he professed. He would, he said, sign a 'cartful of oaths' before he would lose his place. As long as Charles was king he was prepared to serve him to the best of his abilities, which were considerable. He enjoyed administration, negotiation and intrigue, and was prepared to work hard at them. In comparison Middleton and friends were a bunch of amateurs, and he regarded their attempts to govern the country with critical contempt. Clarendon, who hated him, strongly opposed his appointment, but Charles appreciated Lauderdale's abilities and gave him the post.

Clarendon was, however, determined to do something to counter Lauderdale's influence at Whitehall. He therefore proposed the setting up at court of a standing council to advise the King on Scottish affairs – a council consisting of any members of the Scottish privy council who happened to be present, together with six members of the English council. This would mean a permanent English majority. Such a council would not only help nullify Lauderdale's influence, but would also ensure that English interests were always paramount in any formal discussion of Scottish business at Whitehall. Lauderdale strongly opposed the scheme, telling Charles that it would be impossible to keep Scotland loyal and contented if policy there was to be decided by Englishmen. Charles tended to agree with him, but Clarendon had the last word, emphasising the part played by the Scots in the Civil War, and maintaining that only a firm English hand could keep them in order. This argument won the day and the council was set up.

Such, then, was the system of government established at the Restoration. Policy was decided at Whitehall by the King acting with the advice of his Scottish Council on the basis of reports received through his secretary from the commissioner and the other officers of state in Scotland. The King's decisions were then conveyed back to Scotland by the secretary for implementation by the Scottish parliament and privy council. In practice the system did not work well, and broke down completely after just over two years.

The main problem was the poor relationship between the secretary and the ministers in Scotland. Middleton's style of government was to favour direct if not reckless solutions to problems. The shortest cut was always the favoured route. In 1660, for example, the Scottish administration was faced with the task of going through all the legislation passed by the Scottish parliament since 1640 and deciding which acts should be repealed and which allowed to stand. The main burden of this work fell on to the shoulders of a parliamentary committee known as the Lords of the Articles who were responsible for drafting all the acts considered by parliament. The Articles were, it seems, appalled by the magnitude of their task, and they proposed simply to draw up a single measure annulling all the acts passed by the Scottish parliament since 1640. This act had alarming implications since it swept away laws passed by parliament with the King's approval, including all the legislation guaranteeing the existence of the presbyterian church. Nonetheless the act was passed, and Lauderdale criticised Middleton to the King for having assented to a measure which 'must for ever take away all the security which law can give'. In a similar vein he described a parliamentary grant to the King of Scottish revenues of £40,000 a year as 'an inconsiderate act of prodigality or cowardice' which the country could not afford.

Lauderdale's arguments were in vain. The majority of the Scottish council at Whitehall supported Middleton, and Charles went along with them. Middleton and his supporters were nevertheless alarmed by what Lauderdale was doing, and resorted to various stratagems to reduce his influence still further. First, they sent the Earls of Rothes and Glencairn down to London to give a full account of the administration's policies to the King and to other interested ministers. They brought with them a letter from the Scottish parliament containing a dark hint at the mischief wrought in the past by 'too much countenance' being given to 'disaffected persons' and by the 'unstraightness of some public ministers'. Charles received Rothes and Glencairn well and, for the time being at any rate, Lauderdale was effectively by-passed. His position was further weakened when, following the adjournment of the Scottish parliament in July 1661, Middleton himself came to London accompanied by Sir William Primrose, the Clerk Register. A meeting of the Scottish council was called to hear the commissioner's report and, to Lauderdale's astonishment, Middleton wound up his statement by proposing out of the blue that episcopacy should be re-established in Scotland.

This proposal placed Lauderdale in an extremely awkward position. He knew that Charles preferred bishops to presbyteries, but he doubted the practical wisdom of reimposing episcopacy. He had, however, no intention of arguing directly against the move. If he did he might well alienate the King and add weight to the suspicion that he was still at heart a presbyterian sympathiser. In the event, therefore, he temporised, urging caution and consultation. He was, however, opposed by the majority of the council, especially by those ministers who had just come down from Scotland. They could claim to know the popular mood better than did Lauderdale, who had not crossed the border for ten years.

In the end Charles said that he saw that the majority opinion favoured the immediate restoration of episcopacy and ordered it to be done.

Lauderdale had been ignored and outmanoeuvred. Middleton realised that as long as one or two of his party remained at court he had nothing to fear from the secretary. For the time being, however, this advantage was denied to him. Middleton himself had to go to Scotland to prepare for a new session of parliament, and Charles could see no reason why Rothes, Glencairn and the others should stay when there was work to be done in Scotland. Accordingly, at Lauderdale's suggestion, he sent them home and the situation reverted to normal with Lauderdale once more the sole channel of communication between the King and his Scottish ministers. Middleton and his supporters were far from happy with this state of affairs, and the Scottish Privy Council even suggested that Charles should seal all his letters to Scotland with his own hand. But Charles considered this a great trouble to himself as well as a great reflection on his secretary and refused.

Meanwhile in Scotland all seemed well. The bishops were restored without much opposition and with no public disorder. This left the administration free to begin serious consideration of the Scottish Indemnity Act. There had been no Scottish equivalent of the Declaration of Breda so that, in theory at any rate, all Scots guilty of plotting or working against the King during the Civil War and Commonwealth were liable to be charged with treason. Since there was hardly a Scotsman of note who had not at some time fought against the King there could never be any question of proceeding against all traitors. Some advisers, including Lauderdale, urged Charles to offer Scotland the same terms as had been enjoyed by England, but Middleton, who was already engaged in some dubious dealings over the Argyll estates, argued that those who had suffered for their loyalty could only be recompensed by confiscation of the estates of traitors. Accordingly Charles gave him permission to exempt people from the Indemnity Act for any offences committed since 1650, and to fine them sums not exceeding a year's rent.

This was not enough for Middleton and his cronies. They also wanted the power to ban a certain number of those 'most active' in the late rebellion from holding public office. They knew that Lauderdale would oppose such a measure and decided once again to by-pass him. So they sent Sir George Mackenzie of Tarbet to England with two copies of the proposed Indemnity Act. One, to be presented to Lauderdale, omitted the proposal to ban from office. The other, to be presented to the Scottish Council, was complete. On his arrival in London Sir George duly gave Lauderdale the defective copy and the next day, at a full meeting of the Scottish Council, he tabled the full proposals. Lauderdale was furious but impotent. He argued against the new clause but the English majority on the council supported Tarbet, and Charles

*J*ohn Leslie, Lord Rothes in a painting by Schuneman (left)
*and John Maitland, 1st Duke of Lauderdale, 1616–82 in a*
*painting by Huysmans* (right).

took their advice. He also agreed that in future five members of the
Scottish Privy Council, nominated by Middleton, should come to live at
Whitehall. Such a step would have meant not only Lauderdale's personal
eclipse but also a significant down-grading of the office of secretary.

Lauderdale's fortunes were indeed at a low ebb. His advice on
important matters had been consistently ignored and he now found
himself slighted by Tarbet, a man fourteen years his junior. Charles
liked young Mackenzie and would, it was reported, 'close the door'
on Lauderdale when he called Sir George in. The court took their cue
from the King and made a great fuss of the new man. It was therefore
in an optimistic frame of mind that he returned to Scotland. He was
accompanied by the Earl of Newburgh and the twenty-three-year-old
Duke of Richmond, to whom Charles had already given various marks
of his favour including the Garter and a couple of Scottish sinecures.
Tarbet's arrival in Scotland was greeted by much enthusiasm on the part
of his colleagues. They believed that Lauderdale's fall was imminent,
and that their own position was perfectly secure. They were, in fact,
over-confident.

They were also dangerously isolated from Whitehall, for they now
had no agent at court. This did not bother them because they apparently
regarded Richmond as a kind of royal delegate, and seemed to believe
that whatever he suggested was bound to meet with Charles' approval.
With so considerable a figure in Edinburgh they felt they had no need to
check their plans with London. Events in Edinburgh therefore took on a

momentum of their own, with Scottish ministers seizing the initiative in a bout of reckless and intemperate political scheming. The Scots were, without actually realising it, off the leash.

Their schemes still centred round the Indemnity Act. They now had the King's permission to ban up to fourteen individuals from public office, and they decided to use the measure to attack Lauderdale and his supporters. Parliament had the right to name those who were to be banned, and Richmond suggested it ought to be done by a secret ballot, or 'billeting' as it was called. Each member was to write up to twelve names on a piece of paper and place it, unsigned, in a bag. Then the lists were to be examined, the names counted, and the twelve men with the most votes were to be declared incapable of holding public office. The atmosphere was tense and excited. Richmond, Newburgh and others canvassed members, assuring them that it was the King's wish that Lauderdale, among others, should be 'billeted', and distributing lists of all those they wished to see banned. On September 9th, 1662, the votes were cast, and by the end of the day it was clear that the Scottish parliament had banned the King's secretary for Scotland from holding any public office.

It was clearly important that this news should be broken to the King by someone he liked, and who could be trusted to give a favourable account of the whole transaction. Accordingly Middleton entrusted the mission to Tarbet, who was immediately despatched to Whitehall, while a watch was kept on the post at every stage as far south as Durham to make sure that no letter from Scotland containing news of what had happened reached Lauderdale. But the secretary had his own agent in Edinburgh who managed to get a letter to Whitehall before Tarbet arrived. Lauderdale made good use of his advantage. He approached Charles and asked him what would happen if he was billeted. Charles, who had taken it for granted that the measure would only be used against a few fanatical extremists, answered shortly that they would never dare attack his ministers. Hereupon Lauderdale told him what had happened. Charles was taken aback, ascribing it, according to Burnet, to 'the Duke of Richmond's going to Scotland and his being perpetually drunk there'. He told Lauderdale to go and talk to Clarendon who at first refused to believe what he heard, thinking it a put up job by Lauderdale or one of his friends to break Middleton. He eventually told Lauderdale that if Charles allowed it to pass he would never be able to get anyone to serve him and that 'he himself would go out of his dominions as fast as his gout would suffer him'.

Tarbet therefore met a cool reception when he reached court. He wrote to Middleton who, to give him his due, realised what had gone wrong. 'I perceive,' he wrote, 'when none of us are there, we are still at a loss'. The absence of a reliable link with Whitehall had led men of unblemished loyalty to encourage parliament to attack one of the King's chief ministers. They had completely misread the situation. In the first place they had taken it for granted that because Richmond was a personal favourite of the King he was also his political confidant. This was not the case. Richmond had no worthwhile political influence. More fundamentally, they had failed to realise that a parliamentary assault on one of his ministers was bound to be abhorrent to Charles and to all those who had hitherto been their constant supporters at court. Thus the blow which they aimed at Lauderdale rebounded on themselves. It is no wonder that in after years Lauderdale described September 9th as 'St Billeting's Day'.

It was clearly impossible for Charles to trust Middleton and his cronies any longer. He turned instead to Lauderdale who now became the central figure in the Scottish administration. Under his influence certain significant changes were made. Most obviously the Scottish Council at Whitehall was abandoned, and the proposal to send five Scottish councillors south to Whitehall was dropped. These actions had important consequences. The power and influence of the secretary were enormously increased. He was now the only official at Whitehall for the King to consult on Scottish affairs. This meant that his opponents had

*An* illustration from Nicolas de Gueudeville's Atlas Historique *published in 1721 is the only illustration of the Scottish parliament in session.*

127

nobody they could approach. On the other hand, English influence over Scottish affairs vanished at a stroke. From now on the King received advice only from Scotsmen. Clarendon's attempts to establish firm control over Scotland had failed. The disappearance of the council also emphasised the personal nature of Charles' rule over Scotland. 'You govern this poor kingdom yourself,' Lauderdale told him. And it was true.

Lauderdale also, by implication, down-graded the post of commissioner. Middleton was dismissed and was eventually sent off to govern Tangier. Lauderdale did not take the post of commissioner for himself, though it was his for the asking. Instead the Earl of Rothes was appointed. He was a smooth, pliant man and Lauderdale, who had his measure, preferred to remain at court with constant access to the King. It was not until 1669 that he went to Scotland as commissioner, and even then he retained the post of secretary which he was to keep until incapacitated by a stroke in 1680.

Once the dust had settled Lauderdale often seemed complacent. He wrote in August 1663 that he had a good master and cared not 'three skips of a cur tyke' what could be said or done against him. But he never forgot the importance of maintaining a good line of communication with the court. Whenever he was in Scotland he left a deputy at Whitehall who sent him long, detailed reports to keep him in touch with Charles' wishes. He was often accused in his later years of being out of touch with the grievances and aspirations of his fellow Scots, but never of not knowing the King's mind. Thus in 1679, when a Scottish deputation went to Whitehall to complain of the secretary's misdeeds, Charles admitted that they had 'objected many damned things that he had done against them, but there was nothing against his service'. Lauderdale realised better than anybody that success in Scottish politics depended on constant access to the King. He was therefore careful to make sure that he always had the King's ear while his critics were excluded. His long tenure of office is sufficient evidence of his success.

Today, 300 years after Lauderdale's death, Scotland's relations with England are once again a matter of debate. Though circumstances are very different it is still tempting to look at what happened after the Restoration to see if there are any lessons to be learned. It is clear that in 1660, though the union was dissolved and Scotland regained her parliament, the country was still governed from London just as firmly as it had been under the Cromwellian union. And, to take the story forward a few years, as soon as the Scottish parliament tried to assert an independent line on a matter of consequence, it was abolished. Advocates of a Scottish assembly may well see it as a cautionary tale.

# CHAPTER XI

# Jacobitism

ALLAN I. MACINNES

From the deposition of James VII in 1689 to the flight in the heather of his grandson – Charles Edward, 'Bonnie Prince Charlie' – in the summer of 1746, the restoration of the Stewart dynasty was a major preoccupation of Scottish politics, an irritant to successive British governments and a peripheral theme in European diplomacy.

The fluctuating and rarely co-ordinated support of France, Spain, Sweden, the papacy and even Peter the Great of Russia furnished the Jacobite cause with a vital means of finance and prestige. Diplomatic recognition for each of the five Jacobite insurrections – in addition to the major outings of 1689, 1715 and the '45, there were minor flurries in 1708 and 1719 – guaranteed the cause a measure of international respectability. Close surveillance by British governments on known influential Jacobites limited the build-up of military resources, and made foreign arms and money necessary. The deployment of disciplined and professional foreign troops, though limited, contrasted with the Jacobite irregulars.

Yet the whole diplomatic background was fatally flawed. The early eighteenth century was an age of imperial rivalry and nationalist, economic competition among the leading European powers. For the French in particular, Jacobitism was a useful tool with which to embarrass British governments. But they were reluctant to mount and sustain a full-scale invasion fearing that, if the Jacobite cause was successful, the Stewarts would inherit and perpetuate British expansionist policies. Indeed, after the death of Louis XIV, who had been the main sponsor of James VIII, the 'Old Pretender', since 1701, the government of France passed to the Regent Orleans who withheld support from the rising of 1715. In a further effort to gain British recognition for his claim to be heir-apparent to the French throne, Orleans even sent over troops to oppose the Spanish expedition of 1719 in favour of the 'Old Pretender'. He also had the Jacobite court expelled from France. The subsequent re-establishment of the Jacobite court at Rome with pensions from the papacy was essentially a propaganda exercise. For papal support was intended as much to disconcert France as to succour the Catholic Stewarts. No papal recognition was to be afforded to Prince Charles Edward until 1766 – when all his Jacobite pretensions had been subsumed in drunken bewilderment!

Through commercial contacts and embassies noting the movements of money and troops, British governments usually knew in advance about any rising to be mounted with continental support. Indiscretions by rival factions in foreign governments were a further source of information. Most blatantly, when France was attempting to get concerted Spanish and Swedish support for another campaign in 1741, Elizabeth Farnese, Queen of Spain, fearing that her country would thereby become a French satellite, took out an advertisement in the *Amsterdam Gazette* exposing French designs.

Moreover, since British governments were adept at intercepting Jacobite letters through the postal services, undue reliance had to be placed on agents to co-ordinate British mobilisation and continental support for the cause. But all Jacobite agents specialised in self-deception and inept communication. The most devious was probably William Drummond of Balhaldy, *alias* the son and heir to the chief of the outlawed Clan Gregor, whose duplicity R.L. Stevenson has immortalised in *Kidnapped* and its sequel *Catriona*. The cause was further hampered by uncooperative cliques amongst the Jacobite exiles in Paris and Rome. By 1741, the Jacobite leadership in Scotland was afraid to initiate a propaganda campaign in the certainty that their plans for a rising would be leaked to the British government. Ultimately, this lack of liaison, at a time of renewed French initiative under Louis XV, led to a crisis of confidence. Hence, while agents compiled reports exaggerating the support for the Jacobite cause within the British Isles, the Scottish leadership waited for newspapers to authenticate reports of a projected French invasion in 1743.

The final testimony to this lack of concerted campaigning and, indeed, of political realism came in the summer of 1745 when Prince Charles Edward, as the 'Young Pretender', landed on the isle of Eriskay in the Outer Hebrides with seven followers, a ship-load of arms and 4,000 French gold coins. He thereby set aside the prophetic warnings of the Jacobite leadership in Scotland that unless he could bring 6,000 regular troops, arms for 10,000 more and 30,000 French gold pieces, it would mean ruin to himself, to his supporters and to the cause.

Yet, while the lack of adequate foreign backing and continental liaison led to frustration within Jacobite ranks in Scotland, and occasioned the virtual absence of demonstrable military support from English Jacobites, the major risings of 1689, 1715 and the '45 owe their moderate – and albeit initial – degree of success to native Scottish factors.

The appeal of Jacobitism was primarily dynastic: adherence to the hereditary principle of kingship. A further contributory factor was religion. Jacobitism tended to draw the bulk of its support from Scotland north of the Tay, where the population was predominantly episcopalian with scattered pockets of Catholicism in the north-east as also in the western Highlands and Islands. Yet, among the clans, support for their chiefs cut across religious affiliations. During the rising of 1715, William, Earl of Seaforth was the Catholic leader of the Protestant MacKenzies, while the Protestant Angus MacDonald of Glengarry led out his Catholic clansmen.

For the clans, the appeal of Jacobitism was rooted in the traditional values of chiefship and kinship transplanted nationally into support for the royal house of Stewart. As the chief was the protector of the clan localities, so the Jacobite kings were trustees of Scotland. Moreover, dynastic legitimacy was seen as the source of justice, the basis of government. But this genealogical continuity had been broken first by William of Orange in 1689 and then by the establishment of the house of Hanover under George I in 1714. Ultimately, as is evident from the following lines by Alasdair MacDonald, the leading Jacobite poet and Gaelic polemicist of the eighteenth century, the failure of the '45 and the exile of Prince Charles Edward undermined the whole fabric of society:

> We've lost our tiller and our rigging,
> Our sheet-anchor's torn away,
> We've lost our charts, our compass with them,
> Our pole star, our daily guide.

At a more mundane, but pragmatic level, James VII, while still Duke of York, did much to lay the foundations for the overwhelming support of the clans for the cause. Despatched to Scotland to take the heat out of the Exclusion Crisis manufactured in England to debar his succession, as a Catholic, to the throne, James in 1682 instigated a brief respite in the repressive policies pursued towards the clans by central government since the Restoration. Rather than resort to the military option to secure peace and curtail banditry in the Highlands, James preferred to work co-operatively with chiefs and clan gentry to maintain law and order. Following his accession in 1685, clans in the western Highlands and Islands, such as the Camerons, the Macleans and certain branches of the Clan Donald, appealed to the judicious exercise of the royal prerogative to terminate their satellite relationship to the omnipotent Clan Campbell. For successive earls of Argyll, with the active connivance of central government, had expanded their territorial spheres of influence by exploiting the mounting burden of debts encumbering the estates of neighbouring chiefs: debts arising from their clans' increased involvement in national politics since the outset of the seventeenth century compounded by the accumulating fiscal demands of the state since the Restoration. Chiefs were pressured into ceding superiority over their estates and even faced eviction because of the unrivalled ability of the house of Argyll to manipulate legal technicalities. James VII had appeared to have imposed a definite check on such territorial acquisitiveness by having Archibald Campbell, the ninth Earl, executed in 1685. However his peremptory forfeiture was rescinded at the Revolution when his son, Archibald, was restored in full as the tenth Earl. William of Orange's subsequent bestowal of ducal dignities on the chiefs of Clan Campbell served to confirm their emergence as Whig grandees at the outset of the eighteenth century.

In short, Jacobitism before 1707 sought to amend the political direction of Scotland. Following the Treaty of Union, this objective was submerged in the struggle to retain the political identity of Scotland.

Economically, the union was conceived as a treaty to foster free and equal trade between two unequal nations. Scotland, as the weaker partner, suffered a recession that lasted until mid-century and was only partially relieved by grants from Westminster. Indeed, it can be contended that these grants were primarily forthcoming because of Jacobite unrest. Politically, the union was made feasible because aristocratically led factions in pursuit of power and office were prepared to succumb to terms dictated by the English ministry and backed up by the threat of military invasion. However, the consequent subordination of Scotland to the dictates of English ministries and the monopolising of political patronage by their favoured faction made Jacobitism a viable political alternative in Scotland as well as a useful springboard to regain influence for Scottish politicians thrown out of office by any change of ministry in England.

John Erskine, Earl of Mar, who led the rising in 1715, was known as 'Bobbing John'. Having been removed from office as Secretary of State for Scotland at the Hanoverian succession, he was able to play on the Scottish Jacobites' need for a prominent leader. Unfortunately for the cause, Mar's undoubted administrative abilities were not matched by any perceptible military expertise. His unilateral assumption of leadership failed to channel widespread discontent with the Treaty of Union into a successful Scottish rebellion. By the spring of 1716 the rising had petered out and Mar had fled into permanent exile on the continent. For the remaining sixteen years of his life, his flair for intrigue and his constant search for office made him a malign influence within Jacobite circles – especially at the exiled court in Rome – a manipulator rather than co-ordinator of continental support for further risings within the British Isles and, ultimately, in the forlorn hope of attaining a pardon, a paid informant of the British government.

Despite the continuance of widespread discontent with the Treaty of Union, Jacobitism was but one means of protest – albeit the most overtly political – and had to compete with smuggling, the national pastime of Scotland in the early eighteenth century. Moreover, Jacobitism had to face the full weight of religious counter-propaganda, particularly as James VII had been deposed for attempting to set aside constitutional

*The inspiration of Jacobite loyalty. James Francis Edward Stewart, 'The Old Pretender', 1688–1766 (above left), and Charles Edward Stewart, 'The Young Pretender', 1720–88 (above right), both painted by Louis Gabriel Blanchet.*

barriers to secure toleration for his fellow Catholics. James VIII had refused overtures from his half-sister, Queen Anne, to declare himself a Protestant in order to pave the way for his restoration. Furthermore, the Treaty of Union had safeguarded the established position of the Church of Scotland which, in turn, made presbyterian pulpits powerful propaganda organs of government. Thus, presbyterians, disenchanted with the union but dreading the restoration of a Popish king, could only sympathise with, not participate in, the cause.

Within Scotland, therefore, the union was becoming increasingly ingrained as an institutionalised grievance in the course of the eighteenth century. Conversely, the opening up of English and imperial markets not only compensated for the loss of Scotland's traditional trading outlets on the continent but actually led to a measure of economic growth as the century progressed. The combination of presbyterianism and commercial advantage led to militant anti-Jacobitism and the formation of militia units in Edinburgh, Stirling, Dumbarton, Glasgow, Paisley and Ayr, no less ready to fight for the British government and the house of Hanover in 1745 than in 1715. Even within the Highlands, in those areas where presbyterianism had made limited inroads, namely in the shires of Argyll, Ross, Caithness and Sutherland, there was a consistent tendency among the Clans Campbell, Gunn, Mackay, Monro and Ross to support the British establishment. In turn, despite the limited use of foreign troops on either side, the rebellions took on the character of civil wars in Scotland, marked by the militant divergence of opinion among families. Perhaps the most spectacular divergence of opinion was that within the house of Atholl.

John Murray, the first Duke, had hedged his bets in 1689, personally supporting William of Orange but not attempting to prevent the recruitment of his tenantry for the Jacobite cause. A noted, if lukewarm, opponent of the Treaty of Union, he was reconciled to the English ministry and the Hanoverian succession by 1715. However, his eldest son, William, Marquis of Tullibardine, a former officer in the Royal Navy, commanded the Atholl Brigade for the Jacobites in 1715. Although exiled, attainted and debarred from the succession to the dukedom, he was joint-commander in Scotland of the abortive Spanish expedition of 1719. He was again to return from exile in the entourage of Prince Charles Edward in 1745. In the meantime, his brother James, an officer in the British army, had succeeded as second Duke in 1724. Although James played no active part in 1715, he was to return to Scotland in the entourage of William, Duke of Cumberland, in 1746. Two younger brothers, Charles and George, also officers in the British army, commanded regiments in the Atholl Brigade during 1715. Whereas Charles' Jacobite career was terminated by his death in 1720 following a period of imprisonment in London, George returned from exile on the continent to participate in the expedition of 1719. Notwithstanding his pardon of 1724, Lord George Murray rejoined the cause as the brilliant Jacobite commander of the '45. He was opposed by his half-brother, Lord John Murray, who helped raise a clan regiment (the 43rd Highlanders) for the British government in which George's eldest son John, the future third Duke, served as a captain.

Even within the clans there was endemic divergence of opinion by the '45, which amounted to defiance of chiefs. Having cast aside his former neutrality, Norman MacLeod of Dunvegan and Harris declared for the British government towards the end of 1745 and sent a detachment to garrison Inverness. Nonetheless, some of his clan gentry recruited handsomely for the Jacobite cause. More audaciously, William Mackintosh of that Ilk raised a company for the clan regiment of whom all but nine deserted to join the 600 clansmen recruited for the Prince by his wife, Lady Anne Mackintosh.

Jacobitism in Scotland had too many inherent contradictions. The clans formed the bedrock of all risings, bar the hiccough in 1708. Partly this can be attributed to their military tradition. This factor can be overplayed, however. The resolving of clan feuds by recourse to arms had died out in the seventeenth century. Before the battle of Killiecrankie in July 1689, Jacobite officers were particularly concerned that the Highlanders were raw, undisciplined troops who had never seen blood. Technological changes in weaponry had meant that arms were no longer coming off trees and chiefs were increasingly reluctant to meet the expense of providing guns. Want of arms and ammunition, no less than money, greatly hindered the recruitment of clansmen for the Jacobites as for the British government during 1715. Prior to the battle of Prestonpans in September 1745, Donald Cameron of Lochiel was obliged to dismiss 150 of his clansmen for want of arms. At the decisive battle of Culloden in April 1746, ammunition was at such a premium that the Jacobites were confined to twelve rounds while Cumberland's forces were allowed twenty-four.

In truth, clanship placed ultimate priority on the peaceable settlement of land within a hostile environment. The only non-labourers were the clan gentry or tacksmen who acted more as estate managers than as a military caste. The predatory tradition of cattle reiving was largely confined to the most inaccessible districts of the Lochaber region, the Highlands within the Highlands, and practised by freelance cateran (Highland) bands rather than as a clan enterprise – albeit such banditry provided a useful smear against Jacobite clans.

Militarily, the attraction of the Highlands for the launching of risings was that the clan hosts could be readily mobilised by sending round the fiery cross. Moreover, social occasions, notably hunts involving Low-land landlords as well as clan chiefs, provided convenient covers to plot rebellion, as was demonstrated by Mar in August 1715. The difficulties of communication, both geographic and linguistic, circumscribed the capacity of the British government to mount any prompt offensive. Yet, as manifest by the fluctuating nature of clan support in all risings, the further the campaigns progressed from the Highlands the more the appeal of the cause diminished as the clans' traditional territories remained unprotected.

However, the greatest contradiction lay in the attempt of the Jacobite claimants to reconcile their main goal – the English throne – with their military support, which was almost exclusively Scottish. This was par-ticularly evident during the '45. Within one month of Prince Charles Edward raising his standard at Glenfinnan in August, Edinburgh was taken. By levying taxation, the Jacobites began acting as an army of provisional government. The Scottish Privy Council, which was the central intelligence agency as well as the executive pre-union, had been abolished in 1708 to be replaced only by Westminster indifference. Thus, despite previous risings, all police-keeping expedients – such as the militias in the shires supplemented by Independent Companies in the Highlands – had been allowed to lapse. Rather than consolidate in Scotland in the face of peak government inefficiency, the Prince decided he would march on England. This allowed the government forces to regroup on a British basis, permitted civil war to flourish in Scotland

*J*acobite leaders. *John Erskine, 6th Earl of Mar, 1675–1732*
(above left), *pen and wash by Kneller. Lord George
Murray, 1700, son of the 1st Duke of Atholl* (above right).
*John Graham, 1st Viscount Dundee, 1649(?)–89* (below).

and prevented the establishment of any secure bridgehead to await or
encourage foreign intervention.

The initial success of the march to Derby flattered to deceive.
The lack of foreign support undermined the last vestiges of confidence
among English Jacobites, while the Highland character of the army led
to complete failure of identification with the Scots. English matrons
allegedly believed that Cameron of Lochiel ate babies – the only foun-

dation for this rumour was the vampire kiss his grandfather had given an English officer to avoid capture during the Cromwellian occupation of Scotland in the 1650s. By the time of the retreat Jacobite lines of communication had been over-extended. As the campaign was mounted in winter, provisioning was extremely difficult. Both at the front and the rear the Jacobite army was faced with superior English forces under the respective commands of the Duke of Cumberland and General George Wade. The Brigade of Guards stood between the Prince and London. Ultimately, the decision to retire was the result of Scottish pressure as articulated by Lord George Murray according to the campaign journal kept by David Wemyss, Lord Elcho:

> 4,500 Scots had never thought of putting a King upon the English throne by themselves . . . they should go back and join their friends in Scotland and live and die with them.

All Jacobite campaigns were dogged by varying measures of ill-luck and crass incompetence. In 1689, the death of the Jacobite leader, John Graham, Viscount Dundee, neutralised the victory of Killiecrankie. Thereafter, the campaign petered out through the incapacity of Irish officers to manage the clans harmoniously. In 1708, the French-backed invasion was delayed because the 'Old Pretender' caught measles. The fleet eventually arrived off the Firth of Forth, but the appearance of superior forces of the Royal Navy prevented the establishment of a beachhead. On being forced back to France around the north of Scotland and Ireland, the faulty navigation of the admiral caused virtually the whole fleet to founder. Further full-scale invasions launched by the Spanish in 1719 and the French in 1744 were wrecked by storms.

In 1715, Mar, by a disastrous combination of chronic indecision and tactical illiteracy, threw away the overwhelming superiority of the Jacobites over the government forces. Having mobilised around 10,000 men and captured both Inverness and Perth by the end of September, the Jacobites dallied for over a month rather than press home their military advantage over the 4,000 government troops commanded by John Campbell, second Duke of Argyll. While in Perth, no effort was made to secure adequate provisioning, repair arms or erect fortifications – a task eventually entrusted to the enigmatic variations of a French dancing master. No determined effort was made to lay siege to Stirling, the garrison at the cross-roads of Scotland, or to engage openly the government troops who were in no position to absorb or replace any casualties of scale. A detachment under William Mackintosh of Borlum was despatched across the Firth of Forth to liaise with the Scottish Borderers and Northumberland gentry sympathetic to the cause. Instead of effecting a concerted pincer movement on Edinburgh, the Northumberland gentry insisted upon marching into England: a course which ended peremptorily in defeat at Preston after nationalist rivalry had threatened a pitched battle within the Jacobite ranks. In the meantime, Mar prepared to line up against the government troops in November. Although his forces still outnumbered those of the government by a ratio of two-to-one, Argyll was allowed to choose the battleground. At Sheriffmuir, the Jacobite troop formations were drawn up by field-commanders who apparently did not know their left from their right. The battle ended in a draw. Mar having surrendered the initiative, the belated arrival of the 'Old Pretender' in December – courtesy of a French package – led to no tangible result other than a dispiriting six-week conducted tour of Jacobite strongholds in the north-east.

In 1719, the command of the expeditionary forces sent to the Western Isles, reflecting the divisions among Jacobite exiles, was disputed between the Marquis of Tullibardine and George Keith, the Earl Marischal. Excessive delay in Stornoway meant that the government forces had already mobilised under General Joseph Wightman by the time Tullibardine was attempting to rally the clans on the mainland. The government won a decisive victory at Glenshiel in Wester Ross, again helped by the Jacobite tendency to score own goals. Once the Royal Navy had seized and destroyed one Jacobite arsenal at Eilean Donan, the Jacobites themselves destroyed the other at Loch Duich to prevent its confiscation.

In the '45, the only campaign actually led in the field by a Jacobite claimant, the 'Young Pretender' was able to benefit from the military capabilities of Lord George Murray who, in turn, gained and was to retain the confidence of the clan chiefs. Hitherto, Prince Charles Edward's military experience was confined to spectating at the six-day siege of the obscure Italian town of Gaeta when he had not quite attained the age of fourteen. Instead of working through a council of war and giving discretionary power to his field-commanders, the Prince preferred to issue orders imperiously which he expected to be obeyed without equivocation. Although forced to retreat from England against his will in December, morale was still high because of the successful rearguard action fought by Lord George Murray which culminated in the Jacobite victory at Falkirk in January 1746. But a combination of dissension in the ramshackle command structure, failure to take Stirling and the withdrawal of clansmen to protect their traditional territories led to retreat to Inverness and the final slaughter at Culloden in April. Prior to the battle, the Prince attempted an abortive night attack on Cumberland's camp at Nairn at a time when his troops were half-starved and supplies all but run down. The cumulative effect was a near mutiny in Jacobite ranks. One-fifth of the army was incapable of fighting. The tactical ineptitude of the Prince and his chief adviser, the negligent Irish quartermaster Colonel John William O'Sullivan, was amply demonstrated by their

*The disillusioned exile: Prince Charles Edward Stewart in 1785, attributed to Batoni.*

choice of Culloden: a decision which failed to appreciate the irregular nature of the Jacobite troops and the preference of the clan chiefs for a winter guerilla campaign in the Highlands. Chronic vacillation on the part of the Prince exposed his army to a one-hour cannonade of grapeshot, without reply – the Jacobites had no ammunition to match the calibre of their artillery. The demoralised clansmen were then ordered to charge uphill into rifle fire and fixed bayonets!

Each Jacobite failure was marked by government reprisals of varying barbaric degrees, particularly against the clans. After Killiecrankie, the continuance of the clans in a state of military preparedness until 1691 served only to heighten the frustration of William of Orange and his government. Hence, when the MacDonalds of Glencoe – a small clan, much addicted to banditry – failed to take up William's offer of indemnity by January 1st, 1692, they were massacred. In 1708, the ferocious and ill-defined English law of treason was foisted on Scotland in direct breach of the Treaty of Union, a measure which made possible the show trials of Scottish Jacobites in English courts following subsequent rebellions. The greatest measure of leniency came after the rising of 1715, partly because of the widespread Jacobite affiliations of the Scottish nobles and gentry; partly because of the need to establish the house of Hanover; and partly because of the remarkable escape record of imprisoned Scottish Jacobites awaiting trial or execution in England. Following the abortive expedition of 1719 and subsequent rumours of Jacobite plots, the government attempted the pacification of the Highlands by the Disarming Act of 1725 which, like its predecessor nine years earlier, mainly gained compliance from clans favourably disposed to the British establishment. General Wade also began his road programme and attempted to establish an espionage network using renegade clansmen, like Rob Roy MacGregor, as 'supergrasses'.

The greatest severity followed the '45. After establishing a tradition of Highland transvestitism, Prince Charles Edward escaped to France in the summer of 1746, to be followed by many chiefs and gentry. Informing became a growth industry. Captured Jacobites, if they survived imprisonment and the show trials in Carlisle, York and London, were usually shipped off to the plantations. As a sop to English public opinion, heritable criminal jurisdictions – which were mainly the preserve of the Scottish nobility not the clan chiefs – were abolished, as were the military tenures made anachronistic by the commercial changes in landownership since the sixteenth century. The office of Secretary of State for Scotland was also terminated. Further repressive legislation rigorously enforced disarming within the Highlands and banned such cultural trappings as the wearing of kilts and tartan. Speaking the Gaelic language was proscribed.

Clanship was annihilated after the '45. The most telling external contribution was that of the Duke of Cumberland who, having contemplated the wholesale transportation of Jacobite clans, settled instead for a draconian purge of Scottish Gaeldom. That he was but the mouthpiece and avenging agent for the undoubted Scotophobia of the whole political establishment in England affords no defence for his authorising of wanton butchery. The resulting genocide was a major trough for British imperialism. This indiscriminate carnage was carried out by Scottish as well as English officers. The most sadistic – psychologically disturbed from his christening, perhaps – was the Borderer, Captain Caroline Scott.

The more insidious contribution was that of the chiefs themselves. The traditional values of clanship were eroding from the mid-seventeenth century as the chiefs became increasingly assimilated to the British establishment. Their political involvement in Edinburgh and their occasional sojourns to the court in London had led to sporadic absenteeism and an increasing burden of debt which could only be recouped by placing greater emphasis on their individual rights as proprietors to exploit the resources of their estates. The periodic establishment of Independent Companies from the Restoration had served to undermine their traditional role as protectors of the clan territories. The abolition of the Scottish Privy Council in 1708 ended government attempts to run the Highlands in co-operation with the chiefs. The forfeiture of their fathers after the rising of 1715 and their own subsequent restoration had persuaded chiefs like Sir Alexander MacDonald of Sleat and Kenneth MacKenzie, Earl of Seaforth, to abstain during the '45. The chiefs of the Chisholms of Strathglass, the Stewarts of Appin and the MacDonald branches of Clanranald and Glengarry, though sending out contingents of clansmen for the cause, had hedged their bets by staying at home themselves. Indeed, in the midst of the military reprisals following Culloden, John MacDonald of Glengarry attempted unsuccessfully to dissociate himself from the Jacobite involvement of his clansmen. Sir Ludovic Grant of that Ilk actually turned over to the British army those of his clansmen who had escaped the carnage of Culloden. Most crassly, George, Lord Reay, chief of the Mackays, advised Cumberland in his dealings with the Highlanders that:

> . . . it is easier to conquer than to civilize barbarous people.

For at least fifteen years prior to the '45, clansmen were leaving for the Americas. Either they were led from Argyll, the central Highlands and Sutherland by clan gentry seeking to re-establish a traditional lifestyle in Georgia and the Carolinas, or they were the victims of landraids in the Hebrides designed to secure cheap labour for the plantations in the West Indies. Chiefs desiring higher rents from the profits of the thriving trade in black cattle at the expense of their gentry, the clan middlemen, acquiesced in the emigration of the first group. To the second they turned a blind eye.

Culloden, and thereby the ultimate failure of Jacobitism in Scotland, was to provide the psychological escape clause for chiefs ambitious to dispense with the traditional obligations of clanship. Their preference was for absenteeism allied to the 'improvement' of their estates. The ground was now prepared for the Highland Clearances of the later eighteenth century.

# CHAPTER XII

# Scotland's Links with Europe 1600–1800

A. J. G. CUMMINGS

Although situated in the remote north-western corner of Europe, Scotland's links with its continental neighbours have always been strong. Since the Middle Ages, merchants from the east coast ports had been trading to continental Europe and these links were to be strengthened in the seventeenth and eighteenth centuries and were increasingly to involve the west coast ports. Scottish monarchs regularly looked to Europe for their brides. James VI married Anne of Denmark, Charles I, Henrietta Maria of France and Charles II, the Portuguese Princess Catherine of Braganza.

Education and the law also showed strong European influences. Whereas England developed her own highly individual universities and legal system, those of Scotland drew very much on continental models and for much of the period many Scots were still educated abroad. But above all, Scotland has always been noted for its export of manpower. Whether as traders, soldiers or as scholars, Scots have left their native land and often made a considerable impact on their adopted homes.

Down to 1672, overseas trade in Scotland was the monopoly of the royal burghs, holding charters of incorporation from the crown. Within these towns, this privilege was only extended to the members of the merchant guild who, as leading citizens, dominated the town councils. Ties of kinship meant they were often related to many other merchants within their own or indeed other burghs. It was through such links that Protestant ideas had infiltrated Scotland in the sixteenth century. The royal burghs for their part were represented in parliament and in the Convention of Royal Burghs. The latter met regularly, acted as a regulator of the activities of its members and was, on occasion, consulted by the government as a sounding-post for public opinion on economic matters. Thus the merchants represented a commercial élite in Scotland with at least some voice in the running of the kingdom.

By the turn of the seventeenth century the pattern of Scotland's trading links with Europe was fairly clearly established. The principal areas of overseas trade were with Scandinavia and the Baltic, France and the Netherlands. Scandinavia, a short voyage away across the North Sea, was an important source of timber for the Scottish building industry. Considerable forests did exist in the highland areas of Scotland but transport difficulties made it cheaper to import the products of the sawmills of the Norwegian fjords. This trade was of considerable importance to the east coast towns in the first quarter of the seventeenth century. In Dundee approximately one ship in every three was from Norway – usually with timber as its cargo. Norwegian timber continued to be of considerable importance to Scotland throughout the seventeenth and eighteenth centuries.

Sweden too was increasing in importance in Scotland's trading life. Traditionally trade had been with western Sweden. During the sixteenth century though the pattern began to change. Scotsmen were to be found trading in Stockholm and, by the early years of the seventeenth century, this area was an important source of iron for Scottish forges.

The Southern Baltic had, during years of famine in the later sixteenth century, been a source of emergency food supplies for Scotland. The early years of the seventeenth century witnessed a longer series of reasonable harvests in Scotland and less recourse to such supplies. But still, on occasions of shortfall such as that in the period of 1621–23, this area proved of immense benefit to Scotland. In addition to foodstuffs the Southern Baltic provided Scotland with industrial raw materials. Flax and hemp, naval stores such as pitch, tar and rigging as well as potash, copper and timber all featured in cargoes freighted from Danzig in the seventeenth century.

From this pattern of trade it emerges that Scotland's links with Scandinavia were based on her need for primary products. In return its exports were hides, skins, fish, salt and coal, themselves primary products. Demand for Scottish exports was limited and subject to severe competition such as that from the Dutch. As a result, Scotland usually had a balance of payments deficit with the region during the seventeenth century.

With France the relationship was somewhat different. Although the 'Auld Alliance' had been severed in political terms after the Scottish Reformation, economic ties remained for another century. Indeed such was the delight in Edinburgh in 1624 on hearing that Prince Charles was to marry the French Princess Henrietta Maria, that all householders were ordered to light bonfires or suffer a £20 fine.

Trade with France was carried on with two main regions. The first, from the Normandy ports such as Dieppe and Rouen, consisted in the main of vegetable products for which the region was famous, and luxury goods such as manufactures and textiles. Of greater significance, both in bulk and value, was trade with the Biscay area and the ports of La Rochelle and Bordeaux. The Bay of Biscay produced high quality salt by means of evaporation. This was of much better quality than Scottish salt produced by boiling sea water which led to some impurities. French salt was therefore much in demand for the salting of meat and fish and found a ready market in Scotland. Bordeaux provided Scotland with a range of fine wines much appreciated by the middle and upper echelons of Scottish society. Indeed claret, much more than native beverages, was the favourite tipple of well-to-do Scotsmen.

Scottish exports to France emphasised the comparatively rudimentary nature of its economy. The land provided raw wool and skins, and the seas and rivers, salmon and herring. In some areas, such as the Bay of Biscay districts, Scottish cloth might also find a market and occasionally cargoes of coal were finding their way to France. In the main this was a barter trade in the early seventeenth century. Scots disposed of their goods in France and immediately converted them into return cargoes. Scots were later than other Europeans in developing bills of exchange. Lythe has indicated that lack of data precludes a positive answer as to whether or not this trade was to Scotland's overall benefit, but does point out that as time went on wine prices rose much more sharply than fish prices, leading to the possibility that Scotland was more likely to be the loser.

No such difficulties arose over Scottish trade with the Netherlands. The concentrated urban population of this region and its role as an *entrepôt* for the luxury goods of both Europe and the Far East made it one of the major hubs of European trade. The stability and general acceptability of its currency also made the Netherlands a major financial centre. Any surplus in this trade would give Scotland a favourable balance in the most sought after currency in Europe. Business in this sector had developed along familiar lines. Scotland exported primary products in return for luxuries obtainable in the Netherlands.

By the early seventeenth century a new dimension had arisen in Scottish-Dutch trade in the form of coal. Being largely deprived of native resources, the Dutch were forced to import coal. The English government imposed a tax on the export of coal resulting in the Dutch looking not to Tyneside, which would have been geographically much more convenient for them, but to the developing mines around the River Forth. This trade grew so rapidly that by the 1620s some Scots were complaining that not only was coal unobtainable in remoter areas of the country but even in the Forth valley itself. Tales also circulated of Dutch ships queuing in the River Forth to load up with coal. As the Dutch were willing to send ships specifically for coal and, moreover, to pay cash for it, the national interest decreed that little heed was paid to such protestations.

Gradual changes can be detected in the pattern of trade in the seventeenth century. The early years had seen Scots merchants venturing further afield. Despite the protests of the kirk, trade with Catholic Spain began in a small way and Scots were also beginning to penetrate the Mediterranean. Eventually this was to lead to even longer voyages

*The frontispiece to the Journals of the Company of Scotland,
a body which was also involved in the disastrous Darien
scheme in Panama and was frustrated in attempts to establish a
trade in Europe.*

to the developing English colonies in the Americas and significantly to
alter the nature of Scottish overseas trade.

Trade with its traditional partners also came under pressure at this
time. In common with other countries, Scotland suffered in the economic
recession of the second quarter of the century and this was compounded
by civil war at home. The realities of the union of the crowns were
also becoming apparent to the Scots. Foreign policy was no longer a
purely Scottish affair or even a matter where Scottish interests were
paramount. The affairs of England clearly took precedence and Scotland was relegated to the role of unwilling follower. This was clearly
demonstrated in the series of Anglo-Dutch wars first under Cromwell,
then under Charles II. War with her best overseas customer was at best
a short-term interruption to Scottish trade and in the long term, when
trade was reopened, markets were not always regained. The series of
wars with France which followed the accession of William and Mary and
continued into the reign of Queen Anne were much more problematical.
Trade with France was severely disrupted, much to the anger of the
Scots, though it must be stressed that nationalistic economic policies
developed by Colbert had already eaten into Franco-Scottish trade.

The economic and political weakness of Scotland in relation to England is most clearly shown in the attempts of the Scots to raise money to fund the Company of Scotland in 1695. Hostility on the part of the East India Company forced the abandonment of the attempt to raise capital in London. Similar opposition by the Dutch East India Company closed the Amsterdam market. A final attempt to float the scheme in Hamburg was frustrated following pressure from the English consul. The resolution of the Scots to go it alone led to the ill-fated Darien scheme whose failure led to widespread hardship in Scotland. The lack of help from an English government determined not to alienate Spain, in whose territory Darien lay, further fuelled the resentment of Scots against their southern neighbours. The long-term effect of these crises engendered by the disruption of Scottish overseas trade was one of the factors which ultimately convinced people on both sides of the border of the need for a full-scale union of the two countries.

The union of 1707 was of immense significance for Scotland's trade in the long term. English colonies were opened up to Scottish merchants and during the course of the eighteenth century Glasgow merchants made great inroads into the tobacco trade with Virginia. In the years immediately preceding the American War of Independence, tobacco was Scotland's principal import and, because the Navigation Acts prevented the colonies from trading directly with Europe, it was also the principal export. This new commodity re-established links with France and boosted trade with the Netherlands. The French regarded the Scottish market for tobacco as so significant that an agent of the Farmers-General was stationed in the country.

Important as the tobacco trade was to Scotland, it was not the only changing feature of the eighteenth century. The development of the linen industry could not be sustained on home-grown flax and, despite attempts to encourage the native product, one-half of the nation's requirements were still imported, mostly from the Baltic region. From this area also timber and iron were still imported although the latter would soon be replaced as the Scottish iron industry began to develop.

The pattern of economic relations with Europe was seriously disturbed in the wars of the latter years of the eighteenth century. The American War of Independence drastically reduced the re-export trade in tobacco and the French Revolutionary Wars severely affected trade to France and Holland. Scottish trade was turned towards Germany. On the other hand the growing pace of industrialisation in Scotland meant that some of these setbacks were more apparent than real and that the nation could look forward with confidence to the future.

In furtherance of their trade, Scottish merchants not only ventured abroad, but in many cases settled in their adopted countries. By the turn of the seventeenth century many Scots were to be found in

Scandinavia, often as pedlars and sometimes little better than beggars. Trade on a larger scale was conducted by merchants who, given the precarious nature of communications, depended on the trust between one trading partner and another. Personal connections were important in this respect and so an aspiring merchant would often be sent abroad by his family to gain experience in the markets with which the group traded. Often he would find fellow Scots already settled in his destination and perhaps would even register as a burgess in his temporary home. Danzig, Gothenburg and Stockholm all had thriving Scots communities in the early seventeenth century. By the late seventeenth century, as Professor Smout has shown, in principal centres such as Danzig and Stockholm, a few Scots were coming to act as factors for their fellow countrymen and handle an increasing proportion of Scottish trade with the region. But Scots were by no means confined to coastal areas. Many found their way inland and one seventeenth–century estimate, doubtless exaggerated, speaks of thirty thousand Scots in Poland alone. There can be no doubt that Scotsmen were a fairly familiar sight in many areas of northern and eastern Europe in the seventeenth and eighteenth centuries.

Scotland's strongest link with Europe at this time undoubtedly lay with Holland. Trade between the two countries was well established before the seventeenth century and had been limited to a single staple port through which all trade in specified products was required to pass. Such commodities included skins, hides, wool, salt and fish. This restriction had the dual function of making it easier to collect export duties at the royal burghs in Scotland and ensure that no interlopers were breaching the monopoly in the Netherlands. By 1600 the staple was fixed at the port of Campvere (or Veere as it was sometimes known). Here a strong body of Scots settled and the community was run by a Conservator appointed by the Convention of Royal Burghs. The Scots could land their goods duty free and were allowed to run their own affairs and settle their disputes outside Dutch jurisdiction. As a centre for market advice and commercial intelligence, such an organisation could prove invaluable to merchants abroad. Socially, the staple was of considerable importance in the early years of the seventeenth century. It provided accommodation for visiting merchants as well as seeing to the needs of Scottish residents. Spiritual comfort was provided by a resident chaplain. The first minister, Alexander Macduff, was appointed by the Convention in 1612 and from that date until 1799, when the last minister was expelled during the French Revolutionary wars, he and his successors had a considerable effect on the Scots community in Campvere.

The staple itself declined as an economic force during the seventeenth century. After the Restoration, royal interference in the appointment of the Conservator led to a decline in the influence of the Convention. Changes in economic policy in 1672 undermined the monopoly of the royal burghs in overseas trade. Coal, Scotland's principal export to the Netherlands, had never been regarded as a staple product and the bulk of this product was shipped to the major port of Rotterdam. As a result of all of these factors the Scots community in that city grew considerably and by 1700 was reckoned to be around one thousand strong. The staple went into a steady decline in the eighteenth century as the pattern and volume of Scots trade with the Netherlands changed.

Merchants were not the only Scots to seek a living overseas. Life followed art when many Scots followed the pattern of Sir Walter Scott's characters Quentin Durward and Dugald Dalgetty in hiring their swords to foreign employers. After the Reformation and the end of the 'Auld Alliance', the Scots Guard no longer attracted large numbers of Scots to France but the wars of the seventeenth century, particularly the Thirty Years War, proved an adequate substitute. Many Scots flocked to join the armies of Christian IV of Denmark and Gustavus Adolphus of Sweden to further the Protestant cause. At one stage Gustavus had upwards of ten thousand Scots in his ranks. The return of many of these mercenaries to defend the cause of their religion and oppose Charles I under Alexander Leslie had a considerable effect on the early successes of the Covenanters. Even in more peaceful times Scots still went abroad, particularly after 1600 to Holland where, in the Scots Brigade, they formed an important part of the national defence force. Individual Scots made outstanding contributions to foreign employers. James Keith, brother of the Earl Marischal, became a Field Marshal to Frederick the Great of Prussia and Samuel Grieg is credited with the founding of the Russian navy in the second half of the eighteenth century. Not all Scots went abroad voluntarily. The failure of the Jacobite rebellions, particularly those of 1715 and 1745, meant that, for the defeated, exile could result in mercenary work becoming the only way of making a living.

Scots also began to find their way overseas as diplomats. William and Mary used Scots abroad, but during Walpole's tenure of office the numbers declined as he eased them out. By the late 1740s and 1750s their numbers rose again until, by the reign of George III, perhaps one in seven diplomats was a Scot, an indication that Scots were using patronage to the utmost.

During the seventeenth and eighteenth centuries, European influence was increasingly to be seen in Scottish culture. Dutch ideas are said to have influenced the Scottish painter George Jameson in the early years of the seventeenth century, but at that time most Scots preferred to import real Dutch art. In architecture there was the adaptation of older Scottish styles to take account of European developments. Sir William Bruce was responsible for introducing the ideas of Palladio and Inigo Jones to late seventeenth-century Scotland, most notably in his work at Hopetoun House. In the eighteenth century this was taken further by the work of

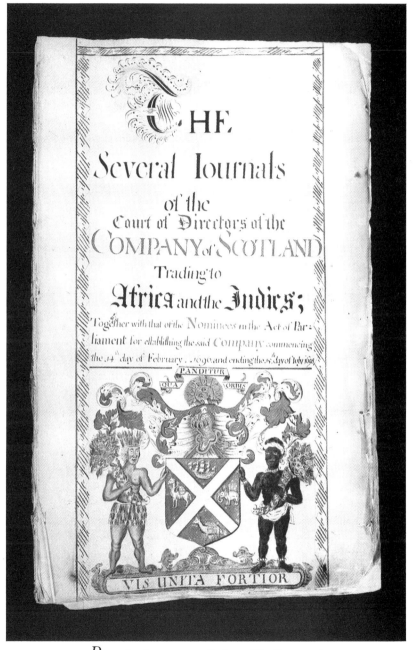

THE

Several Iournals

of the
Court of Directors of the
COMPANY of SCOTLAND

Trading to

Africa and the Indies;

Together with that of the Nominees in the Act of Parliament for establishing the said Company commencing the 14th day of February 1696 and ending the 15th day of July 1698

PANDITUR
QUA ORBIS

VIS UNITA FORTIOR

*P*iranesi's tribute to two notable Scots, Allan Ramsey and
Robert Adam, who visited Rome in the eighteenth century.
The Italian draftsman included the Scots in his imagined
design for tombs of ancient Romans along the Appian Way.

William Adam and especially his son Robert who adapted neo-classical designs and gave them a Scottish dimension. Robert Adam typified the new way of looking at Europe, by going on the Grand Tour as the companion of Charles Hope, younger brother of the Earl of Hopetoun. The Scottish aristocracy, like their English counterparts, were keen on a peaceful penetration of Europe and an absorption of European ideas.

In Scotland this European influence had long been present in higher education. Since the Middle Ages many Scots had gone to universities in France but this declined to some extent after the Reformation. Instead more Scots made their way to Holland, especially to Leyden. Medicine was especially strong at Leyden and Scots who trained there did much to lay the basis for the development of Edinburgh as a centre of British medical education. The reign of William and Mary also gave the link with Dutch universities a distinct political boost and Dutch influence laid the basis for the development and expansion of Scottish universities in the eighteenth century when they were to play an important role in the cultural development of Scotland.

The law of Scotland also owed much to continental influences. Scots lawyers up until the eighteenth century were often educated abroad, particularly in France and Holland where Roman law was part of the basic syllabus. The first systematic examination of Scots law, Stair's *Institutions* published in 1681, showed a distinctly Dutch influence but one adapted to the Scottish situation. From the early eighteenth century legal education in Scotland expanded with the founding of chairs in law at the Universities of Glasgow and Edinburgh. Many aspiring lawyers still studied abroad during the eighteenth century, but, although the need for this had declined, the long-term influence of European ideas was to make Scots law quite different from its English counterpart.

The boost which the universities received from continental influences at the turn of the seventeenth and eighteenth centuries paved the way for the part they were to play in fostering aspects of the Scottish Enlightenment. Here Scotland had a unique part to play in a European movement. Philosophers such as Adam Smith and David Hume exerted an influence far beyond their native land, although the latter did offend the religious establishment to such an extent that it was demonstrated that in eighteenth-century Scotland even Enlightenment had its limits.

The seventeenth and eighteenth centuries were momentous for Scotland. The loss of the last vestiges of political independence left some degree of a vacuum as Scots adjusted to their new role as Britons. In commercial life trade horizons widened, but Europe still had an important part to play. Socially and intellectually, ties with Europe were still strong. Continental ideas inspired many aspects of Scottish life and in return Scots had a distinct influence on European culture in the eighteenth century.

# List of Contributors

JENNY WORMALD is Fellow and Tutor in Modern History at St Hilda's College, Oxford. Her most recent book is *Mary Queen of Scots: A Study in Failure* (paperback 1991).

NORMAN MACDOUGALL is Senior Lecturer in Scottish History at the University of St Andrews. He has published biographies of James III and IV.

RODERICK LYALL is Senior Lecturer in Scottish Literature at the University of Glasgow and the author of several articles in fifteenth- and sixteenth-century literature.

ROGER A. MASON is Lecturer in Scottish History at the University of St Andrews and editor of *Scotland and England 1286–1815* (1987).

KEITH M. BROWN is a Lecturer in History at the University of Stirling. He is the author of *Bloodfeud in Scotland, 1573–1625* (1986).

MICHAEL LYNCH is Senior Lecturer in Scottish History at the University of Edinburgh. His books include *Edinburgh and the Reformation* (1981) and *Scotland: A New History* (1991).

JAMES KIRK is Senior Lecturer in Scottish History at the University of Glasgow and President of the Scottish Church History Society. His most recent book is *Patterns of Reform* (1989).

ALLAN I. MACINNES is Senior Lecturer in Scottish History at the University of Glasgow and the author of *Charles I and the Making of the Covenantor Movement* (1991).

DAVID STEVENSON is Reader in Scottish History at the University of St Andrews. His most recent books are *The Origins of Freemasonry* (1988) and *The First Freemasons* (1988).

JOHN PATRICK was formerly a lecturer in History at Aberdeen College of Education. He now spends his time writing history books, mostly for schools.

A. J. G. CUMMINGS is Lecturer in History at the University of Strathclyde and is currently engaged in research into joint stock companies in England and Scotland in the early eighteenth century.

# Further Reading

# CHAPTER I

## The House of Stewart and its Realm

Rosalind Mitchison's *A History of Scotland* (Methuen, 1970) is a very lively introduction. The same author wrote one of the volumes of the *New History of Scotland* which covers the period, *Lordship to Patronage: Scotland 1603–1745* (reprint, Edinburgh University Press, 1990); the others are Alexander Grant, *Independence and Nationhood: Scotland 1306–1469* (Edward Arnold, 1984) and Jenny Wormald, *Court, Kirk and Community: Scotland 1470–1625* (reprint, Edinburgh University Press, 1991). More detailed coverage is in volumes II and III of the *Edinburgh History of Scotland*: R.G. Nicholson, *Scotland: the Later Middle Ages* (pbk ed. Oliver & Boyd, 1978) and G. Donaldson, *Scotland: James V to James VII* (pbk ed. Oliver & Boyd, 1978), although the first is rather too much informed by the English model, and by a strange beast called the 'medieval constitutionalism of the magnates'. G. Donaldson's *Scottish Kings* (Batsford, 1967) provides brief sketches. More recently, two really satisfying biographies of Stewart kings of Scotland have appeared, both by Norman Macdougall, *James III: A Political Study* (John Donald, 1982) and *James IV* (John Donald, 1989), the latter a very welcome replacement for the enjoyable but lightweight *King James IV of Scotland* by R.L. Mackie (Oliver & Boyd, 1958). A much older study by E.W.M. Balfour-Melville, *James I, King of Scots* (Methuen, 1936), is something of a gift for insomniacs, and very much of the 'English-model' school. Antonia Fraser's *Mary Queen of Scots* (Weidenfeld & Nicolson, 1969) remains the standard biography, though too much of this long and readable book is devoted to the personal drama. G. Donaldson, with his prosopographical study, *All the Queen's Men* (Batsford, 1983), broke exciting new ground in this much trampled subject; while the wealth of publication surrounding the 1987 celebrations of the eternal queen included the delightful *Mary Stewart's People* by Margaret Sanderson (Mercat Press, 1987), and two serious attempts to go beyond the personal and assess her rule, Michael Lynch, ed., *Mary Stewart: Queen in Three Kingdoms* (Basil Blackwell, 1988) and Jenny Wormald, *Mary Queen of Scots: a Study in Failure* (pbk ed. Collins and Brown, 1991). James VI is very much the preserve of Maurice Lee, Jr, with his books *John Maitland of Thirlestane* (Princeton University Press, 1959), *Government by Pen* (University of Illinois Press, 1980) and most recently *Great Britain's Solomon: James VI and I in His Three Kingdoms* (University of Illinois Press, 1990). See also his *The Road to Revolution: Scotland under Charles I, 1625–37* (University of Illinois Press, 1985). The historian whose research first opened up this reign is David Stevenson, with his *The Scottish Revolution* (David & Charles, 1973) and *Revolution and Counter-Revolution in Scotland, 1644–1651* (Royal Historical Society, 1977). Two very recent works are A.I. Macinnes, *Charles I and the Covenanting Movement, 1625–41* (John Donald, 1991) and Peter Donald, *An Uncounselled King: Charles I and the Scottish Troubles, 1637–1641* (1990). Detailed studies of the period are in the articles in J.M. Brown (now Wormald), ed., *Scottish Society in the Fifteenth*

Century (Edward Arnold, 1977), Jenny Wormald, *Lords and Men in Scotland* (John Donald, 1985), K.M. Brown, *Bloodfeud in Scotland, 1573–1625* (John Donald, 1986), and Bruce Galloway, *The Union of England and Scotland, 1603–1608* (John Donald, 1986). The length of this bibliography underlines the point indicated in the Introduction: Scottish scholarship and debate are alive and well.

CHAPTER II
### The Kingship of James IV of Scotland: 'The Glory of All Princely Governing'?

Norman Macdougall, *James IV* (John Donald, 1989); R.L. Mackie, *King James IV of Scotland* (Oliver & Boyd, 1958); Leslie J. Macfarlane, *William Elphinstone and the Kingdom of Scotland, 1431–1514* (Aberdeen University Press, 1985); W. Croft Dickinson, *Scotland from the earliest times to 1603* (revised and edited by A.A.M. Duncan, Oxford University Press, 1977); R.G. Nicholson, *Scotland: The Later Middle Ages* (*Edinburgh History of Scotland*, vol. II: Oliver & Boyd, 1974; reprinted in pbk, 1978); G. Donaldson, *Scottish Kings* (Batsford, 1967); Jenny Wormald, *Court, Kirk and Community: Scotland 1470–1625* (Edward Arnold, 1981); Norman Macdougall, *James III: A Political Study* (John Donald, 1982); David H. Caldwell, ed., *Scottish Weapons and Fortifications 1100–1800* (John Donald, 1981); R.L. Mackie, ed., *The Letters of James the Fourth, 1505–1513* (Scottish History Society, 1953); Trevor M. Chalmers, 'The King's Council, Patronage, and the Governance of Scotland, 1460–1513' (Aberdeen Ph.D. thesis, 1982); Stephen I. Boardman, 'Politics and the Feud in Late Medieval Scotland' (St Andrews Ph.D. thesis, 1990).

CHAPTER III
### The Court as a Cultural Centre

Richard Firth Green, in *Poets and Princepleasers: Literature and the English Court in the Late Middle Ages* (University of Toronto Press, 1980), argues for the importance of aristocratic patronage in an English context. John MacQueen gives a Scottish perspective in '*The Literature of fifteenth-century Scotland*', in J.M. Brown, ed., *Scottish Society in the Fifteenth Century* (Edward Arnold, 1977), cf. also R.J. Lyall, 'Politics and Poetry in Fifteenth and Sixteenth Century Scotland' (*Scottish Literary Journal* 3 (2) December 1976 (5–29).

CHAPTER IV
### 'Scotching the Brut': The Early History of Britain

The best introduction to Geoffrey of Monmouth and his subsequent influence on British historiography is T.D. Kendrik, *British Antiquity* (Methuen, 1950); on sixteenth-century English historiography, see F.J. Levy, *Tudor Historical Thought* (California University Press, 1967); and William Haller, *Foxe's 'Book of Martyrs' and the Elect Nation* (Jonathan Cape, 1967). On Scotland, a mine of relevant information is provided by Arthur H. Williamson, *Scottish National Consciousness in the Age of James VI* (John Donald, 1979); and in the same author's 'Scotland, Antichrist and the Invention of Great Britain', in John Dwyer et al., ed., *New Perspectives on the Politics and Culture of Early Modern Scotland* (John Donald, 1982). For some European comparisons, see the essays by various hands in Orest Ranum, ed., *National Consciousness, History and Political Culture in Early Modern Europe* (Johns Hopkins University Press, 1975). See also Roger Mason's

'Politics, History and National Myth in 16th century Britain', in Roger Mason, ed., *Scotland and England 1286–1815* (John Donald, 1987), pp.60–84.

# CHAPTER V

## The Nobility of Jacobean Scotland 1567–1625

On the nature of aristocratic power see Jenny Wormald, *Lords and Men in Scotland: Bonds of Manrent 1442–1603* (John Donald, 1985) and Keith M. Brown, *Bloodfeud in Scotland 1573–1625: Violence, Justice and Politics in an Early Modern Society* (John Donald, 1986). For the economic history of the nobility see Keith M. Brown, 'Aristocratic Finances and the Origins of the Scottish Revolution', *The English Historical Review*, civ (1989), 46–87; Keith M. Brown, 'Noble Indebtedness in Scotland from the Reformation to the Revolution', *Historical Journal*, 62 (1989), 260–75; and also useful is Keith M. Brown, 'The Price of Friendship; the "well affected" and English Economic Clientage in Scotland before 1603', in R.A. Mason, ed., *Scotland and England 1286–1800* (John Donald, 1987). The religious attitudes and loyalties of the nobility are discussed by Jenny Wormald, '"Princes" and the regions in the Scottish Reformation', in Norman Macdougall, ed., *Church, Politics and Society: Scotland 1408–1929* (John Donald, 1983); Keith M. Brown, 'In search of the godly magistrate in Reformation Scotland', in *The Journal of Ecclesiastical History*, 40, (1989), 553–81; Keith M. Brown, 'The Making of a *Politique*; the Counter Reformation and the Regional Politics of John Eighth Lord Maxwell', in *The Scottish Historical Review*, lxvi (1987), 151–75; Maurice Lee Jr, 'King James's Popish Chancellor', in Ian S. Cowan and D. Shaw, eds., *The Renaissance and Reformation in Scotland* (Scottish Academic Press, 1983). On the nobility and the towns see Keith M. Brown, 'Burghs, Lords and Feuds in Jacobean Scotland', in Michael Lynch, ed., *The Early Modern Town in Scotland* (Croom Helm, 1987). Edward J. Cowan, 'The Darker Version of the Scottish Renaissance: the Devil and Francis Stewart', in Cowan and Shaw, eds., *Renaissance and Reformation* is a good insight into the cultural interests of the nobility. Finally, for the political context see Jenny Wormald, *Court, Kirk and Community: Scotland 1470–1625* (Edward Arnold, 1981), and the more old-fashioned G. Donaldson, *Scotland: James V to James VII* (Oliver & Boyd, 1971); Maurice Lee Jr, *John Maitland of Thirlstane and the Foundation of Stewart Despotism in Scotland* (Princeton University Press, 1959), and by the same author *Government by Pen: Scotland under James VI – I* (University of Illinois Press, 1980).

# CHAPTER VI

## The Scottish Early Modern Burgh

Two recent works devoted to the development of the Scottish town, M. Lynch, ed., *The Early Modern Town in Scotland* (Croom Helm, 1987) and M. Lynch, M. Spearman and G. Stell, eds., *The Scottish Medieval Town* (John Donald, 1988), reflect the substantial amount of recent research on urban history before 1700. The forthcoming new edition of the *Historical Atlas of Scotland*, edited by P.G.B. McNeill and D.E.R. Watt, will also have substantial new material on burghs, settlement and trade. Additionally, there are three essays covering the period before 1700 in the collection edited by G. Gordon and B. Dicks, *Scottish Urban History* (Aberdeen University Press, 1983) and one essay in the important collection edited by R.A. Houston and I. Whyte, *Scottish Society, 1500–1800* (Cambridge University Press, 1989), which includes a full set of tax rolls for all the royal burghs in the sixteenth and seventeenth centuries. The most useful of the older works is probably W.M. Mackenzie, *The Scottish Burgh* (Oliver & Boyd, 1949) and there are two useful introductions to the two volumes edited by G.S. Pryde for the Scottish History Society, *Ayr Burgh Accounts, 1534–1624* (1937) and *Court Book of Kirkintilloch, 1658–1694* (1963). For Glasgow, the best studies remain T.C. Smout's two articles, 'The Development and Enterprise of Glasgow, 1556–1707', *Scottish Journal of Political Economy*, vii (1962) and 'The Glasgow Merchant Community in the Seventeenth Century', *Scottish Historical Review*, xlvii (1968); the one recent detailed study of Edinburgh is M. Lynch's *Edinburgh and the Reformation* (John Donald, 1981).

CHAPTER VII

## Reformation and Revolution, Kirk and Crown 1560–1690

J. Buckroyd, *Church and State in Scotland 1660–1681* (John Donald, 1980); J.K. Cameron, *The First Book of Discipline* (The Saint Andrew Press, 1972); I.B. Cowan, 'The Five Articles of Perth', in D. Shaw, ed., *Reformation and Revolution* (The Saint Andrew Press, 1967); I.B. Cowan, *The Scottish Covenanters, 1660–88* (Gollancz, 1976); G. Donaldson, *Scotland: James V to James VII* (Oliver & Boyd, 1965); G. Donaldson, *All the Queen's Men* (Batsford, 1983); G. Donaldson, *The Faith of the Scots* (Batsford, 1990); W. Ferguson, *Scotland 1689 to the Present* (John Donald, 1968); W. Ferguson, *Scotland's Relations with England* (John Donald, 1977); J. Kirk, *The Second Book of Discipline* (The Saint Andrew Press, 1980); J. Kirk, *Patterns of Reform* (T&T Clark, 1989); M. Lee, *Government by Pen* (University of Illinois Press, 1980); M. Lee, *The Road to Revolution* (University of Illinois Press, 1985); W. Makey, *The Church of the Covenant, 1637–44* (John Donald, 1979); D. Stevenson, *The Scottish Revolution, 1637–44* (David and Charles, 1973); D. Stevenson, *Revolution and Counter-Revolution in Scotland, 1644–1651* (Royal Historical Society, 1977); Jenny Wormald, *Court, Kirk and Community: Scotland 1470–1625* (Edward Arnold, 1981).

CHAPTER VIII

## Covenanting, Revolution and Municipal Enterprise

D. Stevenson, *The Scottish Revolution 1637–44* (David & Charles, 1973); M. Lynch, ed., *The Early Modern Town in Scotland* (Croom Helm, 1986); R.A. Mason, 'The Aristocracy, Episcopacy and the Revolution of 1638', in T. Robertson, ed., *Covenant, Charter and Party* (Aberdeen University Press, 1989).

CHAPTER IX

## The Century of the Three Kingdoms

Anglo-Scottish links are analysed in William Ferguson, *Scotland's Relations with England: A Survey to 1700* (John Donald, 1977), and Anglo-Irish relations in J.C. Beckett, *The Making of Modern Ireland, 1603–1923* (Faber & Faber, 1966), which is an excellent introduction. The attitude of the Covenanters to union is discussed in David Stevenson, *The Scottish Revolution, 1637–44* (David & Charles, 1973) and David Stevenson, *Revolution and Counter-Revolution in Scotland, 1644–51* (Royal Historical Society, 1977). The complex interrelationships of all three kingdoms are a major theme in David Stevenson's *Scottish Covenanters and Irish Confederates: Scottish-Irish Relations in the Mid-Seventeenth Century* (Ulster Historical Foundation, 1981); and David Stevenson's 'Cromwell, Scotland and Ireland', in J.S. Morrill, ed., *Cromwell and the English Revolution* (Longmans, 1990), 149–80. B.P. Levack, *The Formation of the British State: England, Scotland, and the Union, 1603–1707* (OUP, 1987) is an important analysis, while C. Russell, *The Causes of the English Civil War* (OUP, 1990) and *The Fall of the British Monarchies, 1637–1642)* (OUP, 1991) represent a significant re-thinking of the origins of the mid-seventeenth-century upheavals in a fully British context.

CHAPTER X
## A Union Broken? Restoration Politics in Scotland

There is no detailed modern account of Scottish politics in the reign of Charles II. W.C. Mackenzie, *Life and Times of John Maitland, Duke of Lauderdale* (Kegan Paul, 1923) is dated, but W. Ferguson, *Scotland's Relations with England* (John Donald, 1977), G. Donaldson, *Scotland: James V to James VII* (Oliver & Boyd, 1965), R. Mitchison, *Lordship to Patronage: Scotland 1603–1746* (Edward Arnold, 1983) and B.P. Levack, *The Formation of the British State: England, Scotland and the Union* (Oxford, 1987) put events into perspective. J. Buckroyd, *The Life of James Sharp* (John Donald, 1987) gives an episcopal view. G. Burnet, *History of his own Time* (various editions) and Sir George Mackenzie, *Memoirs of the Affairs of Scotland* (Edinburgh, 1821) give detailed contemporary accounts.

CHAPTER XI
## Jacobitism

W.A. Speck, *The Butcher: The Duke of Cumberland and the Suppression of the '45* (Basil Blackwell, 1981); A.J. Youngson, *The Prince and the Pretender: A Study of the Writing of History* (Croom Helm, 1985); F.J. McLynn, *The Jacobite Army in England, 1745: The Final Campaign* (John Donald, 1983); P. Hopkins, *Glencoe and the End of the Highland War* (John Donald, 1986); A. & H. Taylor, eds., *The Stuart Papers at Windsor* (John Murray, 1989).

CHAPTER XII
## Scotland's Links with Europe 1600–1800

T.C. Smout, *A History of the Scottish People, 1560–1830* (Collins, 1969) remains the best overall view of Scottish social history in the early modern period. Bruce Lenman, *An Economic History of Modern Scotland* (Batsford, 1977), examines the period after 1660. T.C. Smout, ed., *Scotland and Europe 1200–1850* (John Donald, 1986) contains some very useful material. Trade in the seventeenth century is dealt with by S.G.E. Lythe, *The Economy of Scotland in its European Setting, 1550–1625* (Oliver & Boyd, 1960) and T.C. Smout, *Scottish Trade on the Eve of the Union, 1660–1707* (Oliver & Boyd, 1963). The role of the merchant community is dealt with in T.M. Devine, 'The Merchant Class of the larger Towns in Scotland in the Seventeenth and Eighteenth Centuries', in G. Gordon and B. Dicks, eds., *Scottish Urban History* (Aberdeen University Press, 1983). The early chapters of G. Donaldson, *The Scots Overseas* (Robert Hale, 1966) indicate the role of Scots in Europe, and the law and medicine are examined in A.C. Chitnis, *The Scottish Enlightenment* (Croom Helm, 1976).

# Index

Numbers in **bold** refer to illustrations

# Illustration Acknowledgements

Mansell/Alinari 13; Mansell Collection 14; by gracious permission of her Majesty the Queen 16; History Today Archives 19; Royal Commission on Ancient Scottish Monuments 20; History Today Archives 21; Scottish National Portrait Gallery 22; History Today Archives 24; Mansell Collection 27; by courtesy of Sir David Ogilvie and the National Library of Scotland 30; Royal Scottish Museum 35; Royal Commission on Ancient Scottish Monuments 37; Bodleian Library, Oxford 41; from *A Concise History of Scotland* by Fitzroy Maclean (Thames & Hudson, 1970) 44; by permission of the Master and Fellows of Magdalene College, Cambridge 47; from *Historia Regum Britannia* of Geoffrey of Monmouth (Longman, 1929) 50; History Today Archives 53; from *The Buik of the Croniclis of Scotland* by Hector Boethius (Longman 1858) 56; by permission of the Master and Fellows of Corpus Christi College, Cambridge 58; Scottish National Portrait Gallery 64; History Today Archives 67; Scottish National Portrait Gallery 69, 70; History Today Archives 74; A.F. Kersting 77; History Today Archives 79, 85; Mansell Collection 86, 91; Scottish National Portrait Gallery 92; Mansell Collection 95; Mitchell Library, Glasgow 98; Mansell Collection 102; Scottish National Portrait Gallery 105 (left); The People's Palace (Glasgow Museums & Art Gallery) 105 (right); History Today Archives/Ashmolean Museum, Oxford 109; Mansell Collection 110, 115; National Library of Scotland 116; History Today Archives 120; Scottish National Portrait Gallery 125 (left); National Portrait Gallery, London 125 (right); Royal Scottish Museum 127; National Portrait Gallery, London 133 (left and right); Scottish National Portrait Gallery 136; National Portrait Gallery, London 139; from *The Scottish World* ed. Harold Ovel et al. (Thames & Hudson, 1981) 145; from *Scotland's Story* by Tom Steel (Collins, 1984) 149.